PAPERBACK SONGS

ELVIS

D0720911

PROPERTY OF
HIGH POINT PUBLIC LIBRARY
HIGH POINT, NORTH CAROLINA

PROPERTY OF
HIGH POINT PUBLIC LIBRARY
HIGH POINT, NORTH CAROLINA

MELODY LINE, CHORDS AND LYRICS
FOR KEYBOARD • GUITAR • VOCAL

781.66
L581E

HAL•LEONARD®

ISBN 0-7935-7342-4

For all works contained herein:
Unauthorized copying, arranging, adapting, recording or public performance is an infringement of copyright.
Infringers are liable under the law.

Visit Hal Leonard on the internet at http://www.halleonard.com

Elvis and Elvis Presley are registered trademarks of
Elvis Presley Enterprises, Inc., Copyright © 1997.

This publication is not for sale in
the E.C. and/or Australia
or New Zealand.

7777 W. Bluemound Rd. P.O. Box 13819 Milwaukee, WI 53213

Welcome to the PAPERBACK SONGS SERIES.

Do you play piano, guitar, electronic keyboard, sing or play any instrument for that matter? If so, this handy "pocket tune" book is for you.

The concise, one-line music notation consists of:

MELODY, LYRICS & CHORD SYMBOLS

Whether strumming the chords on guitar, "faking" an arrangement on piano/keyboard or singing the lyrics, these fake book style arrangements can be enjoyed at any experience level – hobbyist to professional.

The musical skills necessary to successfully use this book are minimal. If you play guitar and need some help with chords, a basic chord chart is included at the back of the book.

While playing and singing is the first thing that comes to mind when using this book, it can also serve as a compact, comprehensive reference guide.

However you choose to use this PAPERBACK SONGS SERIES book, by all means have fun!

CONTENTS

6 Ain't That Loving You Baby
7 All Shook Up
10 Always on My Mind
12 An American Trilogy
18 Any Way You Want Me
20 Anything That's Part of You
22 Are You Lonesome Tonight?
24 As Long As I Have You
26 (You're So Square) Baby, I Don't Care
28 Baby, Let's Play House
30 Big Boss Man
15 A Big Hunk O' Love
32 Bitter They Are, Harder They Fall
38 Blue Christmas
40 Blue Hawaii
35 Blue Moon of Kentucky
42 Blue Suede Shoes
44 Bossa Nova Baby
46 Burning Love
48 Can't Help Falling in Love
50 Change of Habit
52 Charro
54 Clean Up Your Own Back Yard
58 Crying in the Chapel
60 Don't
62 Don't Ask Me Why
64 Don't Be Cruel (To a Heart That's True)
67 Don't Cry Daddy
70 Don't Leave Me Now
72 Doncha' Think It's Time?
74 Fame and Fortune
76 Flaming Star
78 Follow That Dream
80 Fool
82 (Now and Then There's) A Fool Such As I
84 For the Good Times
86 G.I. Blues
88 Girls! Girls! Girls!
91 Good Luck Charm
94 Good Rockin' Tonight
98 Green Green Grass of Home
100 Hard Headed Woman
102 The Hawaiian Wedding Song (Ke Kali Nei Au)
104 Heartbreak Hotel
106 Help Me Make It Through the Night
108 His Latest Flame
114 Hound Dog
116 I Beg of You
111 I Feel So Bad
118 I Got Stung
124 I Gotta Know
126 I Need Your Love Tonight
128 I Want You, I Need You, I Love You

130 I Was the One
132 I'm Leavin'
134 I'm So Lonesome I Could Cry
136 I've Got a Thing About You, Baby
138 I've Lost You
121 If I Can Dream
140 If You Talk in Your Sleep
142 In the Ghetto (The Vicious Circle)
148 It Hurts Me
150 It's Now or Never
152 Jailhouse Rock
145 Kentucky Rain
154 King Creole
156 Kissin' Cousins
159 Little Sister
162 Lonely Man
164 Love Me
183 Love Me Tender
166 Loving You
168 Mary in the Morning
170 Mean Woman Blues
172 Memories
174 A Mess of Blues
176 My Baby Left Me
178 My Boy
180 My Way
184 One Broken Heart For Sale
186 One Night
188 (There'll Be) Peace in the Valley (For Me)
190 The Promised Land
196 Puppet on a String
198 Return to Sender
200 Rock-A-Hula Baby
193 Separate Ways
202 She's Not You
204 Spinout
206 Steamroller (Steamroller Blues)
208 Stuck on You
210 Surrender
216 Suspicious Minds
218 (Let Me Be Your) Teddy Bear
220 That's All Right
222 Too Much
213 Treat Me Nice
224 T-R-O-U-B-L-E
228 Unchained Melody
230 Until It's Time for You to Go
232 Viva Las Vegas
236 Walk a Mile in My Shoes
238 Way Down
243 Wear My Ring Around Your Neck
246 The Wonder of You
248 You Don't Have to Say You Love Me
250 You're the Devil in Disguise
240 You've Lost That Lovin' Feelin'

AIN'T THAT LOVING YOU BABY

Words and Music by CLYDE OTIS
and IVORY JOE HUNTER

Copyright © 1959 by Elvis Presley Music, Inc.
Copyright Renewed and the interest of Clyde Otis
assigned to Elvis Presley Music (Administered by R&H Music)
International Copyright Secured All Rights Reserved

ALL SHOOK UP

Words and Music by OTIS BLACKWELL
and ELVIS PRESLEY

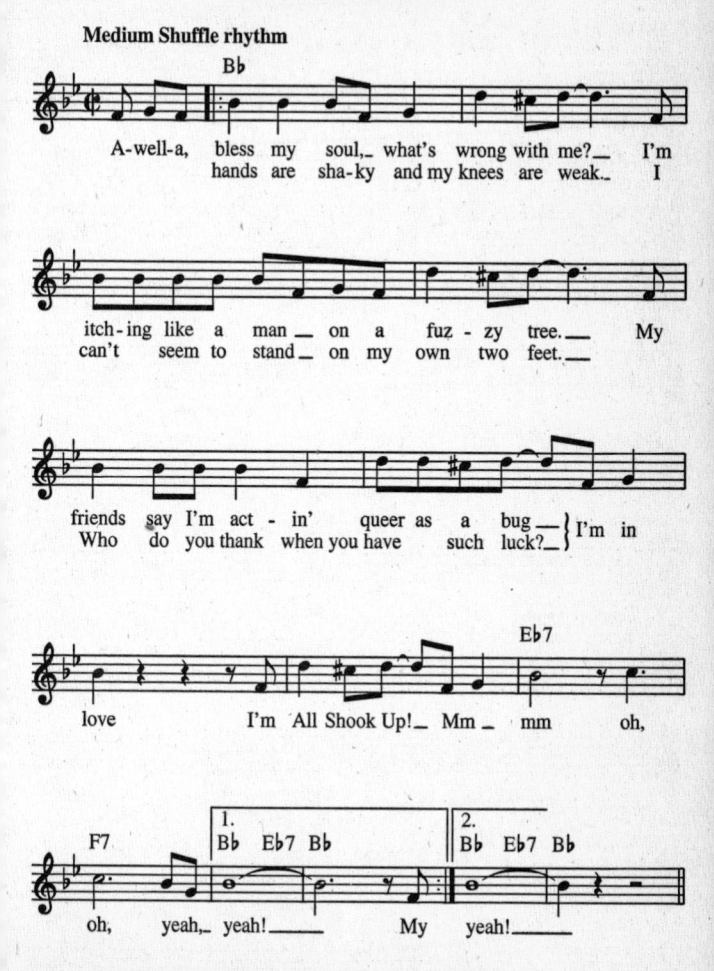

Copyright © 1957 by Shalimar Music Corporation
Copyright Renewed and Assigned to Elvis Presley Music (Administered by R&H Music)
International Copyright Secured All Rights Reserved

E♭7
Please don't ask what's on my mind, I'm a
tongue gets tied when I try to speak, my
B♭7
lit - tle mixed up but I'm feel - in' fine. When I'm
in - sides shake like a leaf on a tree. There's
E♭7
near that girl that I love best, my
on - ly one cure for this soul of mine, that's to
F7
heart beats so it scares me to death!
have the girl that I love so fine!
She
B♭
touched my hand, what a chill I got, her
kiss - es are like a vol - ca - no that's hot! I'm

proud to say she's my but - ter - cup,. I'm in love! I'm
Eb7
All Shook Up! Mm mm oh,
F7
1.
Bb Eb7 Bb
2.
Bb
oh, yeah, yeah! My yeah! I'm
Eb7
F7
All Shook Up! Mm mm oh, oh, yeah,
Bb
Eb7
yeah! I'm All Shook Up! Mm mm oh,
F7
Bb
oh, yeah, yeah! I'm All Shook Up!

ALWAYS ON MY MIND

Words and Music by WAYNE THOMPSON,
MARK JAMES and JOHNNY CHRISTOPHER

© 1971,1979 SCREEN GEMS-EMI MUSIC INC. and BUDDE SONGS INC.
All Rights Controlled and Administered by SCREEN GEMS-EMI MUSIC INC.
All Rights Reserved International Copyright Secured Used by Permission

To Coda
1.
C D7 G C D
Mind.) you were Al-ways On My_ Mind.
2.
G C D G D/F♯ Em G/D
Mind. Tell me,
C G/B Am Am7/D
tell me that your sweet love_ has-n't died.
G D/F♯ Em G/D C G/B
Give me, give me one more chance to keep you sat-is-
Am D7 G D.C. al Coda
fied, sat - is - fied.
CODA
G D/F♯ Em G/D C G/D
Mind. (Instrumental)
Am D7 G D.C. and Fade
You were Al-ways On My Mind.

AN AMERICAN TRILOGY

By MICKEY NEWBURY

Copyright © 1971 by Acuff-Rose Music, Inc.
All Rights Reserved Used by Permission

F♯dim7
C
Am
fros - ty morn - ing, look a - way, look a - way, look a -
Dm7
G7
C
F
C
way Dix - ie - land.
Glo - ry, glo - ry hal - le - lu -
F
jah glo - ry, glo - ry hal - le -
C
E7
lu - jah glo-ry, glo - ry hal-le -
Am
G
F
Dm7
lu - jah His truth is

Dm7/G G7 Am F Dm C
march - ing on.
(Instrumental)
So hush, lit - tle chil - dren, don't you
Gm7 C
cry you know you dad - dy's
Am F C
bound to die. But
Am7 Fmaj7 Dm7
all my trials, Lord
G7 C
soor be o - ver.

A BIG HUNK O' LOVE

Words and Music by AARON SCHROEDER
and SID WYCHE

Copyright © 1959 by Elvis Presley Music, Inc.
Copyright Renewed and Assigned to Elvis Presley Music (Administered by R&H Music)
and Rachel's Own Music (Administered by A. Schroeder International Ltd.)
International Copyright Secured All Rights Reserved

G N.C.
Now you could spare a kiss or two and
But I ain't greed - y ba - by, all I
C7
still have plen - ty left.
want is all you got.
Oh, no, no, ba - by.
G
I ain't ask - in' much of you.
D7
Db7
Just a big - a big - a big - a hunk o'
C7
G
love will do.
1.
2.
You're just a
I got a
G N.C.
wish - bone in my pock - et.
I got a

G N.C.
rab-bit's foot 'round my wrist. And I'd have

G N.C. G N.C.
ev - 'ry - thing my luck - y charms could bring if you

G N.C. G N.C. G N.C.
gim-me just one sweet kiss, oh, no no no no no no,

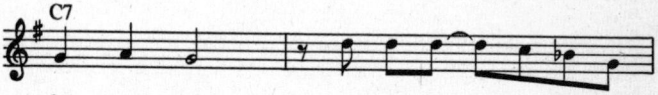
C7
ba - by. I ain't ask - in' much of

G D7 D♭7
you. Just a big-a big-a big-a hunk o'

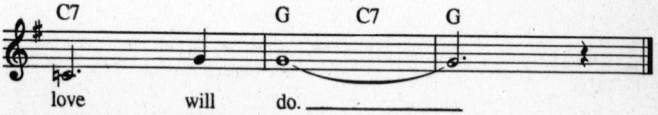
C7 G C7 G
love will do.

ANY WAY YOU WANT ME

Words and Music by CLIFF OWENS
and AARON SCHROEDER

Copyright © 1956 by Chappell & Co. and Rachel's Own Music
(Administered by A. Schroeder International Ltd.)
Copyright Renewed
International Copyright Secured All Rights Reserved

F
C
In your hands my heart is clay, to
F
C
take and mold as you may.
D7
I'm what you make me; you've on - ly to take me, and
G7
C
in your arms I will stay. I'll be a fool or a
Am
F
G7
wise man; my dar - ling, you hold the
C
C7
F
F♯dim7
key. Yes, An - y Way You Want Me, well,
C
G7
1.
C
G7
that's how I will be.
2.
C
F
C
be, I will be.

ANYTHING THAT'S PART OF YOU

Words and Music by
DON ROBERTSON

Copyright © 1962 by Gladys Music, Inc.
Copyright Renewed, Assigned in the United States in 1991 to
Don Robertson Music Corporation, P.O. Box 4141, Thousand Oaks, CA 91359
International Copyright Secured All Rights Reserved

Bb7
Eb
know you don't love me an - y -

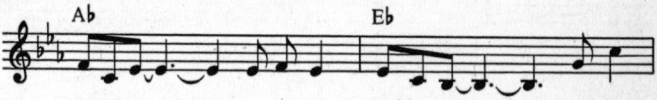
Ab
Eb
more to go on need-ing you know-ing

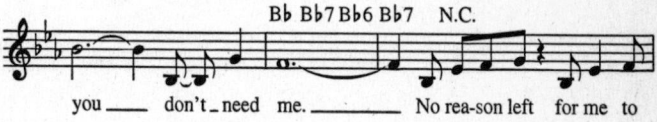
Bb Bb7 Bb6 Bb7 N.C.
you don't need me. No rea-son left for me to

Eb Ebmaj7 Eb7
Ab
live. What can I take, what can I give,

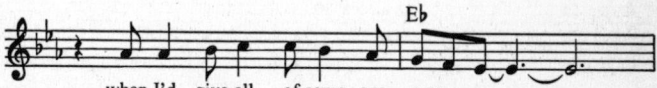
Eb
when I'd give all of some-one new

Bb
Bb7
Eb Ab
Eb
for An-y-thing. That's Part Of You.

ARE YOU LONESOME TONIGHT?

Words and Music by ROY TURK
and LOU HANDMAN

TRO - © Copyright 1926 (Renewed) Cromwell Music, Inc. and Bourne Co., New York, NY
International Copyright Secured
All Rights Reserved Including Public Performance For Profit
Used by Permission

C7
F
chairs in your par - lor seem emp - ty and
Cm/E♭
D7
bare? Do you gaze at your door - step and
G7
F♯7
G7
C
pic - ture me there? Is your heart filled with
C7B♭dim7 D7
pain, shall I come back a - gain? Tell me,
G7
1.
C D7♭9
dear, Are You Lone - some To - night?
G7
2.
C F Fm C
Are You night?

AS LONG AS I HAVE YOU

Words by FRED WISE
Music by BEN WEISMAN

Copyright © 1958 Gladys Music, Inc.
Copyright Renewed, Assigned to Chappell & Co. and Erika Publishing
International Copyright Secured All Rights Reserved

F F7 B♭ Am Dm
You. Let's think of the fu - ture, for -
C♯dim7 Dm Dm7 G7
get the past. You're not my first love but
C7 F Dm
you're my last. Take the love that I bring, 'cause I'll
B♭ C7 Gm7 C7
have ev - 'ry-thing As Long As I Have
1.
F
You. Let the
2.
F
You.

(You're So Square)

BABY, I DON'T CARE

Words and Music by JERRY LEIBER
and MIKE STOLLER

© 1957 (Renewed) JERRY LEIBER MUSIC and MIKE STOLLER MUSIC
All Rights Reserved

C C7 F
new, But no one else can
F#dim7 G7
love me like you do. I
C F C F
don't know why my heart flips; I on - ly know it does.
C F C F
I won - der why I love you, babe, I
C C7 F
guess it's just be - cause you're so square,
G7 N.C. C F7 C
And, Ba - by, I Don't Care.

BABY, LET'S PLAY HOUSE

Written by
ARTHUR GUNTER

Copyright © 1954 (Renewed) by Embassy Music Corporation (BMI)
and Excellorec Music, a division of AVI Music Publishing Group, Inc.
All Rights Administered Worldwide by Embassy Music Corporation
International Copyright Secured All Rights Reserved

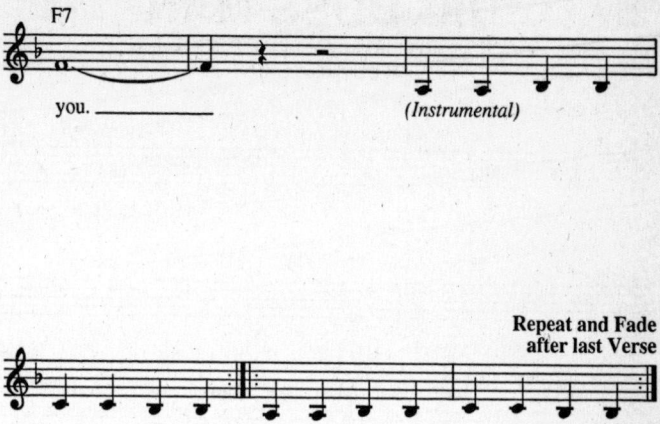

Additional Lyrics

3. This is one thing, baby
   What I want you to know:
   Come on back and let's play a little house
   So we can do what we did before.
   Now, baby, come, *etc.*

4. Listen, I'm telling you, baby,
   Don't you understand?
   I'd rather see you dead, little girl,
   Than to be with another man.
   Now, baby, come, *etc.*

BIG BOSS MAN

Words and Music by AL SMITH
and LUTHER DIXON

Copyright © 1960, 1967 by Conrad Music, a division of Arc Music Corp.
Copyright Renewed
International Copyright Secured All Rights Reserved

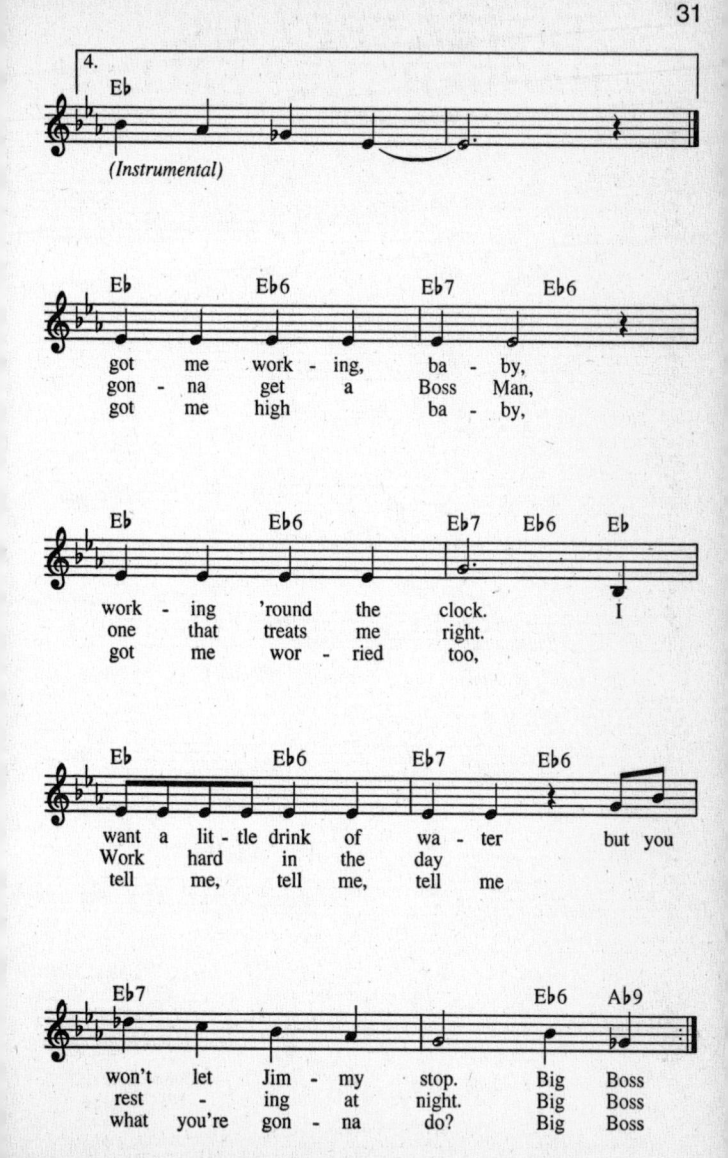
4.
Eb
(Instrumental)
Eb Eb6 Eb7 Eb6
got me work - ing, ba - by,
gon - na get a Boss Man,
got me high ba - by,
Eb Eb6 Eb7 Eb6 Eb
work - ing 'round the clock. I
one that treats me right.
got me wor - ried too,
Eb Eb6 Eb7 Eb6
want a lit - tle drink of wa - ter but you
Work hard in the day
tell me, tell me, tell me
Eb7 Eb6 Ab9
won't let Jim - my stop. Big Boss
rest - ing at night. Big Boss
what you're gon - na do? Big Boss

BITTER THEY ARE, HARDER THEY FALL

Words and Music by
LARRY GATLIN

© 1973 TEMI COMBINE INC.
All Rights Controlled by COMBINE MUSIC CORP. and Administered by EMI BLACKWOOD MUSIC INC.
All Rights Reserved International Copyright Secured Used by Permission

Bb Ab Eb
hall.
Bb
Here come the tear - drops; Bit - ter They
F7 Bb
Are, Hard - er They Fall.
Bbsus Bb7 Bb Bb7
She caught me
Eb Bb7 Eb
ly - in', then
Bb Bbsus
she caught a train.
Bb C7
Then I caught a fe - ver
C7sus C7
walk - in' home in the
Cm7 Ab C7
rain.

F7
Bb
But it's o - ver and un - done;
Bb7
Eb
she's left me once and for all.
Bb7
Eb
Here comes the
Bb
F7
tear - drops; Bit - ter They Are,
Bb
Bb7
Hard - der They Fall.
Eb
Bb
Here come the tear - drops;
F7
Bit - ter They Are, Hard - er They
Eb
Fall.
(Instrumental)
Bb

BLUE MOON OF KENTUCKY

Words and Music by
BILL MONROE

Copyright © 1947 by Peer International Corporation
Copyright Renewed
All Rights Reserved Used by Permission

G7
C7
tuck - y, to keep on shin - ing,
G
shine on the one that's gone and left me blue.
D7
G
I said Blue Moon Of Ken -
G7
C7
tuck - y to keep on shin - ing, shine
G
D7
on the one that's gone and left me blue.
G
G7
C
Well, it was on one moon - light
C7
G
G7
night, stars shin - in' bright,

C
C7
whis - per on high
G
D7
love said good - bye; Blue
G
G7
Moon Of Ken - tuck - y, keep on
C7
G
Gdim
shin - ing, shine on the one that's
D7
1.
G
A7
gone and left me blue.
D7
2.
G C7 C♯dim7 G
I said Blue

BLUE CHRISTMAS

Words and Music by BILLY HAYES
and JAY JOHNSON

Copyright © 1948 PolyGram International Publishing, Inc.
Copyright Renewed
International Copyright Secured All Rights Reserved

C7
Christ-mas, that's cer - tain. And when that
F
blue heart-ache starts hurt - in', You'll be
Am7♭5 D7 Am7♭5 D7 Gm
do - in' all right, with your Christ - mas of
Bdim7 C7
white, but I'll have a blue, Blue
1.
F
2.
F
Christ-mas. I'll have a Christ-mas.

BLUE HAWAII

from the Paramount Picture WAIKIKI WEDDING

Words and Music by LEO ROBIN
and RALPH RAINGER

Copyright © 1936, 1937 (Renewed 1963, 1964) by Famous Music Corporation
International Copyright Secured All Rights Reserved

Bb Bb7#5 Eb
Come with me while the
Bb C7
moon is on the sea. The night is young
Cm7/F F7 F7b9
and so are we.
Bb Eb Bb
Dreams come true in Blue Ha - wa - ii
G7#5 C7 F7
and mine could all come true this mag - ic
Bb Eb/Bb 1. Bb F7 2. Bb
night of nights with you. you.

BLUE SUEDE SHOES

Words and Music by
CARL LEE PERKINS

Copyright © 1955 by Carl Perkins Music, Inc.
Copyright Renewed
All Rights Administered by Unichappell Music Inc.
International Copyright Secured All Rights Reserved

N.C.
F7
slan-der my name all o-ver the place;
drink my ci-der from my old fruit jar;
N.C.
F7
Do an-y-thing that you want to do, but
uh-uh, hon-ey, lay off of my shoes.
B♭7
3
Don't you step on my Blue Suede
F
C
Shoes. You can do an-y-thing but lay
B♭
1.
F B♭7
off of my Blue Suede Shoes.
F C N.C.
2.
F B♭7 F F7♯9
Well, you can Shoes.

BOSSA NOVA BABY

Words and Music by JERRY LEIBER
and MIKE STOLLER

© 1962 (Renewed) JERRY LEIBER MUSIC and MIKE STOLLER MUSIC
All Rights Reserved

bout to have my - self a fit."
ain't got time to think."
find my - self an - oth - er cat."
G
Am/G G
Bos - sa No - va,
Bos - sa
Am/G G
G7
C7
No - va.
(Instrumental)
1.,2.
3.
G
G
G
I said,
I said,
Bos - sa
Am/G
G
No - va,
Bos - sa
Am/G
G
G
No - va.
(Instrumental)
C7
G
Repeat and Fade

BURNING LOVE

Words and Music by
DENNIS LINDE

Moderate Boogie-Rock

Lord Al-might - y, I feel my temp - 'ra-ture ris -
Oo - ee I feel my temp - 'ra-ture ris -
It's comin' clos - er, the flames are now lick - in' my bod -

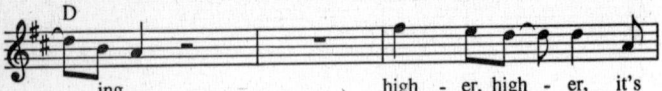

- ing, high - er, high - er, it's
- ing, help me, I'm flam - in', it
- y, won't you help me? I

burn - ing thru to my soul.
must be a hun-dred and nine.
feel like I'm slip-pin' a - way.

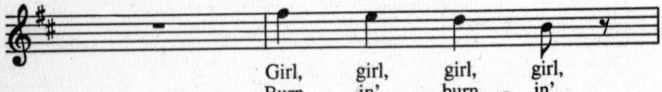

Girl, girl, girl, girl,
Burn - in', burn - in',
It's hard to breathe

you've gone and set me on fire,
burn - in' and noth-in' can cool me,
and my chest is a heav - in',

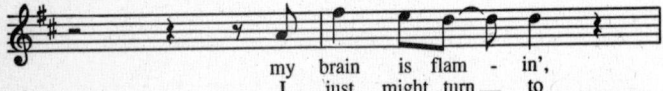

my brain is flam - in',
I just might turn to
Lord have mer - cy, I'm

I don't know which way to go.
smoke but I feel fine.
burn-in' a hole where I lay.

© 1972 TEMI COMBINE INC.
All Rights Controlled by COMBINE MUSIC CORP. and Administered by EMI BLACKWOOD MUSIC INC.
All Rights Reserved International Copyright Secured Used by Permission

Bm
A
Your
Your
'Cause your
kiss - es lift me high -
G
Bm
A
- er, like the sweet song of a choir,
G
Bm
A
and you light my morn - in' sky
G
A7sus
D
with burn - in' love.
1.,2.
3.
G
A7sus
With burn - in' love.
D
G
With just a
D7
G
Repeat and Fade
hunk-a, hunk-a burn-in' love.
With just a

CAN'T HELP FALLING IN LOVE

from BLUE HAWAII

Words and Music by GEORGE DAVID WEISS, HUGO PERETTI and LUIGI CREATORE

Copyright © 1961 by Gladys Music, Inc.
Copyright Renewed and Assigned to Gladys Music (Administered by Williamson Music)
International Copyright Secured All Rights Reserved

Am E7 Am E7
Like a riv - er flows sure - ly to the sea,
Am E7 Am F♯dim7
dar - ling, so it goes some things are meant to
Gm C7 F Am Dm
be. Take my hand, take my
B♭ F C7
whole life too, for
B♭ C Dm Gm
I Can't Help Fall - ing In
F/C C7 1. F C7 (D.C.) 2. Dm
Love with you. you. For
B♭ C7 Dm Gm
I Can't Help Fall - ing In
F/C C7 F
Love with you.

CHANGE OF HABIT

Words by BUDDY KAYE
Music by BEN WEISMAN

Bright Rock

G Em G

If you're in old hab - its, set in your old
if you're in the hab - it, let your tem - per
if you're in the hab - it of put - ting peo - ple

Em Am D7

ways, chang - es are a - com - in' 'cause
fly, when you talk with peo - ple who
down, just be - cause they're dif - f'rent, from the

F D7 G

these are chang - ing days. And if your head is
don't see eye to eye. And if you don't be -
wrong side of town. Well, don't count on an - y

C Cm

in the sand, while things are go - in' on,
lieve that there's a new - er world a - head, } what you
med - als, son, they're pin - ning down on you,

Bm Em Bm Em

need, what you need,

C D7 To Coda

what you need is a Change Of

Copyright © 1970 by Gladys Music, Inc.
Copyright Assigned to Gladys Music (Administered by Williamson Music)
International Copyright Secured All Rights Reserved

1.
G
Em
G
D7
Hab - it.
Now
2.
G
F
Hab - it.
A Change Of Hab - it,
G
a change of out - look,
a change of
C
G
heart,
you'll be all right.
F
The halls of dark - ness
our souls will
G
C
o - pen,
it's nev - er late
D7
to see the light.
D.C. al Coda
So
CODA
G
Hab - it.
Repeat and Fade
B♭ C

CHARRO

Words and Music by BILLY STRANGE
and SCOTT DAVIS

Copyright © 1969 by Gladys Music, Inc.
Copyright Assigned to Gladys Music (Administered by Williamson Music)
International Copyright Secured All Rights Reserved

B♭
But which road leads you to to - mor -
But how much more time can you bor -
But will you live to see to - mor -
C
D
To Coda
1.
Am
row,
row,
row,
Char - ro.
B♭(no5)
2.
Dm
(Instrumental)
A7
Now at a sin - gle mo-ment your past grows dim.
Dm
One thought goes rac - ing a - cross your mind;
D7
Gm
You ride to meet the wom-an you stole from him, Oh,
E7
no, Char - ro, don't go, Char - ro, don't
D.C. al Coda
go.
CODA
Repeat and Fade
D
Am

CLEAN UP YOUR OWN BACK YARD

Words and Music by SCOTT DAVIS
and BILLY STRANGE

Copyright © 1969 by Elvis Presley Music, Inc.
Copyright Assigned to Elvis Presley Music (Administered by R&H Music)
International Copyright Secured All Rights Reserved

F7
Bb7
Clean Up Your Own Back Yard,
F
Don't you hand me none of your line;
C7
Clean Up Your Own Back Yard,
Bb7
F
Bb
You tend to your bus-'ness, I'll tend to mine.
1.,2.
To Verses 2.& 3.
F7 Bb7 B7 C7
3.
F
Fine
Verse 2
F
Drug-store cow-boy crit - i - ciz - in',
act - in' like he's bet-ter than you and
Bb7
me;
Stand-in' on the side-walk su - per - vis - in',

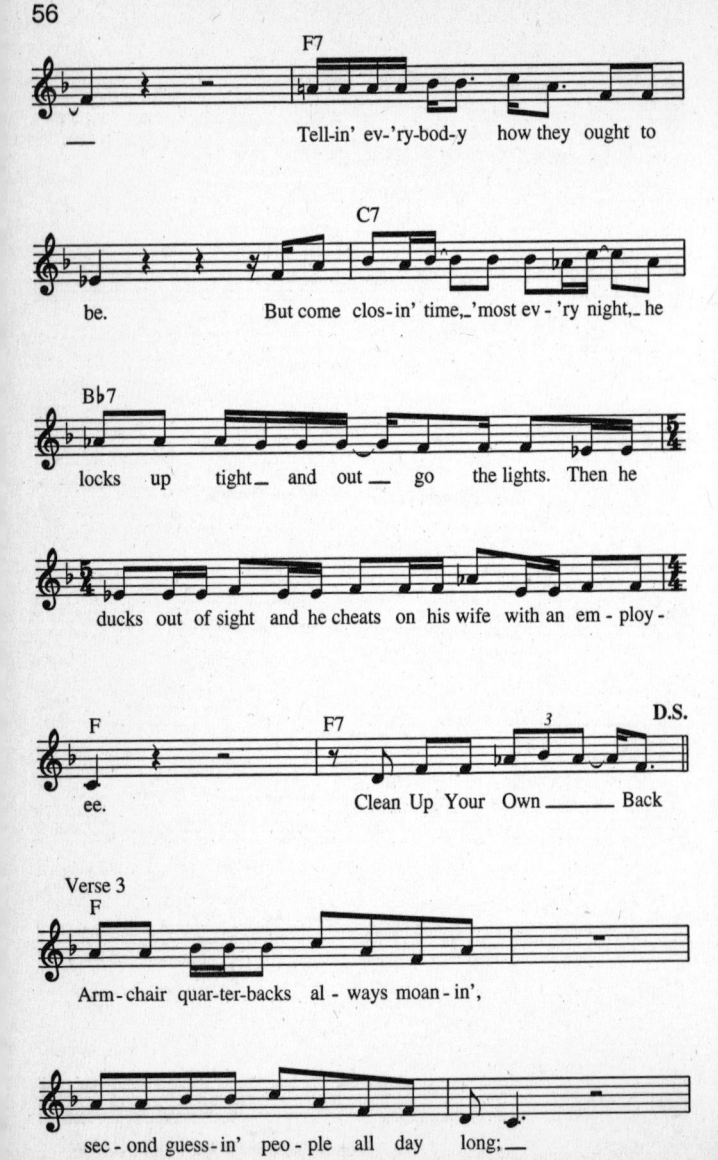
F7
Tell-in' ev-'ry-bod-y how they ought to
C7
be. But come clos-in' time,_ 'most ev-'ry night,_ he
B♭7
locks up tight_ and out_ go the lights. Then he
ducks out of sight and he cheats on his wife with an em-ploy-
F
ee.
F7
3
D.S.
Clean Up Your Own_____ Back
Verse 3
F
Arm-chair quar-ter-backs al-ways moan-in',
sec-ond guess-in' peo-ple all day long;_

B♭7
Push-in', pull-in', hang-in' on in,
F7
al-ways mess-in' where they don't be - long. But when you
C7
get right down to the nit - ty grit - ty,
B♭7
is - n't it a pit - y that in this big cit - y, not
one lit-tle bit-ty man-'ll ad - mit he could-a been a lit-tle bit
D.S. al Fine
F
F7
3
wrong.
Clean Up Your Own Back

CRYING IN THE CHAPEL

Words and Music by
ARTIE GLENN

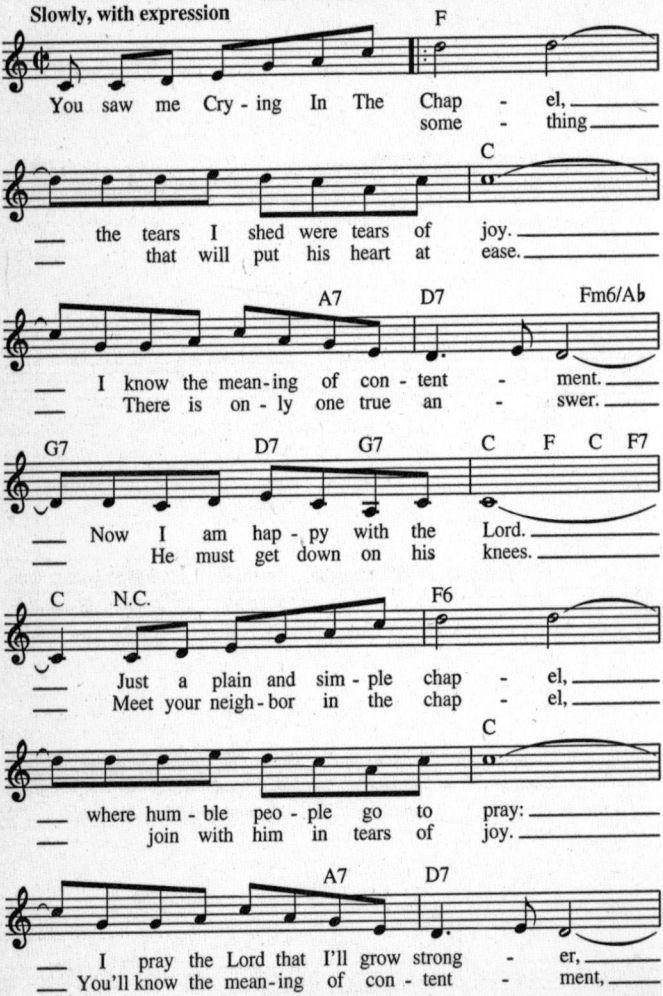

Copyright © 1953 by Unichappell Music Inc.
Copyright Renewed
International Copyright Secured All Rights Reserved

G7 D7 G7 C F C F7
as I live from day to day.
then you'll be hap - py with the Lord.
C C7 F Fm6 A♭/G♭
I've searched and I've searched, but
You'll search and you'll search but
C A7 D7 Am7 D7
I could-n't find no way on earth to gain peace of
you'll nev - er find no way on earth to gain peace of
G7 N.C. F6
mind. Now I'm hap - py in the chap - el,
mind. Take your trou - bles to the chap - el,
C
where peo - ple are of one ac - cord.
Get down on your knees and pray.
A7 D7 Fm6/A♭
We gath - er in the chap - el,
Your bur - dens will be light - er,
1.
G7 D7 G7 C Dm7
just to sing and praise the Lord.
and you'll sure - ly find the
G7 N.C.
2.
C F C F7 C
Ev - 'ry sin - ner looks for way.

DON'T

Words and Music by JERRY LEIBER
and MIKE STOLLER

© 1957 (Renewed) JERRY LEIBER MUSIC and MIKE STOLLER MUSIC
All Rights Reserved

G7
if you think that I Don't mean
C7 Bdim7/C C7
ev - 'ry word I'm say - ing,
F C7 F F7
Don't, Don't, Don't feel that
B♭ C7 F
way. I'm your love and
Am Dm Gm7
3
yours I will stay.
C7 N.C. F F7
This you can be - lieve; I will nev - er
B♭ Gm7 C7 F Dm
leave you, heav - en knows I won't.
Gm7 C7sus C7 F B♭7 F
Ba - by, Don't say Don't.

DON'T ASK ME WHY

Words by FRED WISE
Music by BEN WEISMAN

Copyright © 1958 Gladys Music, Inc.
Copyright Renewed, Assigned to Chappell & Co. and Erika Publishing
International Copyright Secured All Rights Reserved

C G7 C N.C.
love I dreamed a - bout, but it's the
D7 G7
kind that I can't live with - out.
N.C. C D♯dim7
You're all I'm long - ing for; don't say good-
Dm7 G7 Dm7 G7 Dm7
bye. I need you more and more;
G7 1. C A♭7
Don't Ask Me Why.
G7 N.C. 2. C Fm C
I'll go on Why.

DON'T BE CRUEL

(To a Heart That's True)

Words and Music by OTIS BLACKWELL
and ELVIS PRESLEY

Copyright © 1956 by Unart Music Corporation and Elvis Presley Music, Inc.
Copyright Renewed and Assigned to Elvis Presley Music (Administered by R&H Music)
International Copyright Secured All Rights Reserved

G7
C
you I'm think-ing of.
C
Don't stop think-ing of me, don't make me feel this
walk up to the preach-er, and let us say, "I
C7
F
way. Come on o-ver here and love me, you
do." Then you'll know you have me, and I'll
C
Dm7
know what I want you to say. Don't Be Cruel
know I'll have you too. Don't Be Cruel
G7
C
to a heart that's true. Why
to a heart that's true. I don't
F
G7
F
should we be a-part? I real-ly love you,
want no oth-er love, Ba-by it's just

G7
1.
ba - by, cross my heart. Let's
you I'm think - ing
2.
C
Dm7
of. Don't Be Cruel
G7
C
to a heart that's true. Don't Be
Dm7
G7
C
Cruel to a heart that's true.
C7
F
G7
I don't want no oth - er love
F
G7
C
C7
Ba - by, it's just you I'm think-ing of.

DON'T CRY DADDY

Words and Music by
MAC DAVIS

© 1969 SCREEN GEMS-EMI MUSIC INC. and ELVIS PRESLEY MUSIC
All Rights Controlled and Administered by SCREEN GEMS-EMI MUSIC INC.
All Rights Reserved International Copyright Secured Used by Permission

PROPERTY OF
HIGH POINT PUBLIC LIBRARY
HIGH POINT, NORTH CAROLINA

Em
Dad-dy, please don't cry.
A
G
A
Dad-dy, you've still got me and lit-tle Tom - my. To-
D
G
geth - er we'll find a brand new mom - my.
D
Dad - dy, Dad - dy, please laugh a - gain.
A7
Dad - dy, ride us on your back a - gain. Oh,

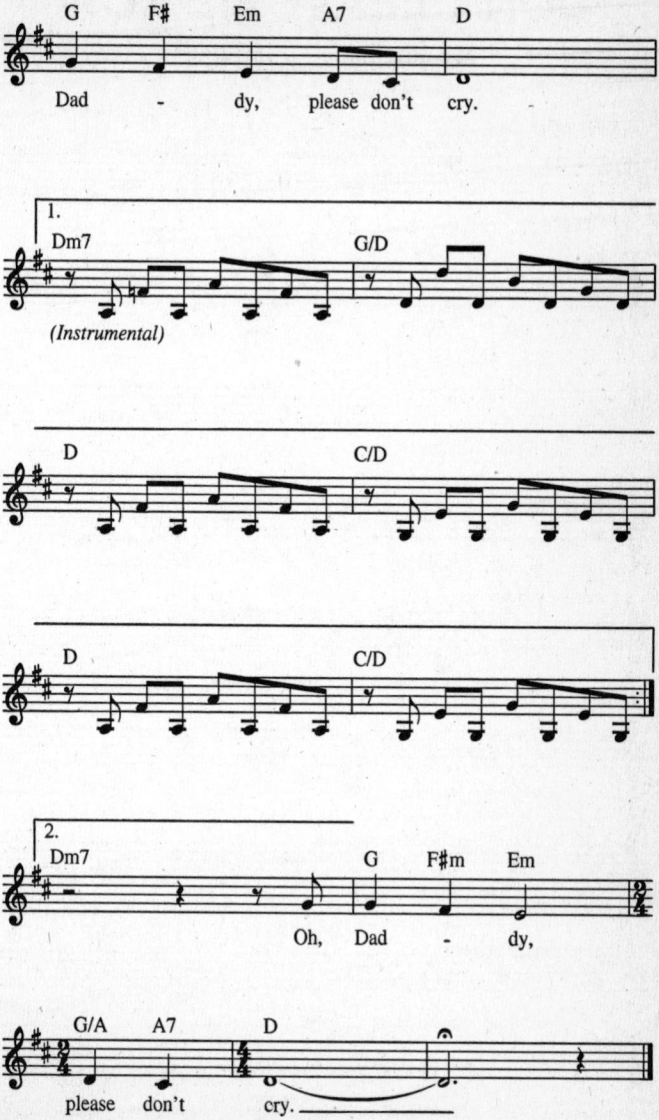
G F♯ Em A7 D
Dad - dy, please don't cry.
1.
Dm7 G/D
(Instrumental)
D C/D
D C/D
2.
Dm7 G F♯m Em
Oh, Dad - dy,
G/A A7 D
please don't cry.

DON'T LEAVE ME NOW

Words by AARON SCHROEDER
Music by BEN WEISMAN

Copyright © 1957 Gladys Music, Inc.
Copyright Renewed, Assigned to Chappell & Co. and Rachel's Own Music
(Administered by A. Schroeder International Ltd.)
International Copyright Secured All Rights Reserved

C N.C. F
What good is dream - ing
C F7
if I must dream all a - lone by my -
C N.C. D7
self? With - out you, dar - lin',
G7 N.C.
my dreams would just gath - er dust like a book on a
C
shelf. Come fill these arms,
C7 F
that long to hold you.
G7
Don't close your eyes to my plea.
1.
N.C. C Ab7
Oh, don't you leave me now!
2.
G7 N.C. C F7 C
Don't Leave Me Now, now!

DONCHA' THINK IT'S TIME?

Words and Music by CLYDE OTIS
and WILLIE DIXON

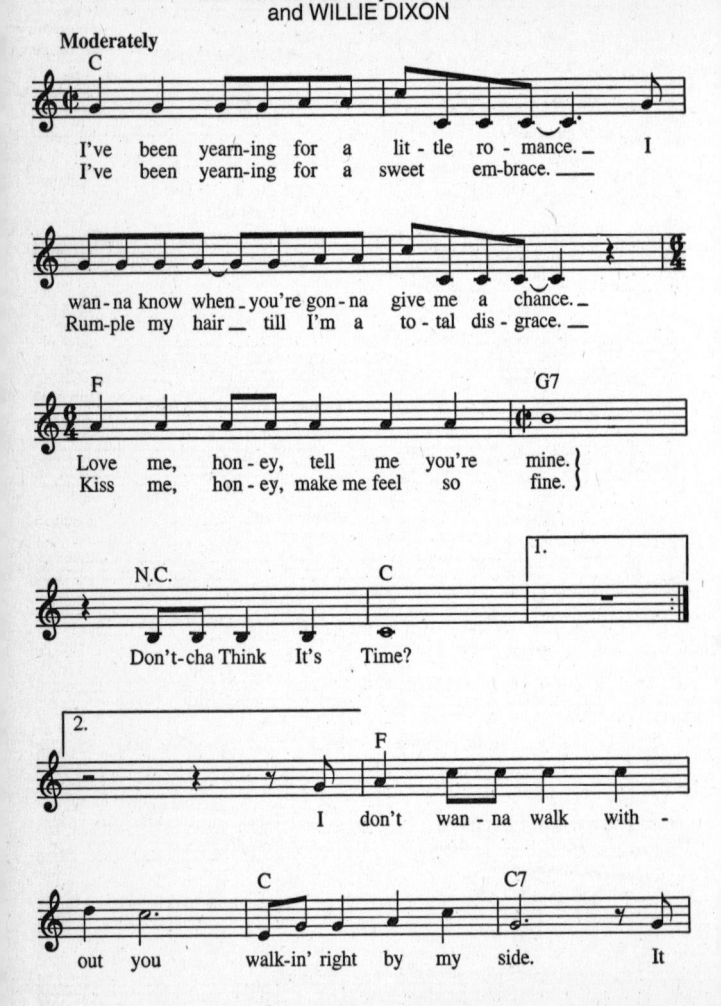

Copyright © 1958 by Elvis Presley Music, Inc.
Copyright Renewed and Assigned to Elvis Presley Music (Administered by R&H Music)
International Copyright Secured All Rights Reserved

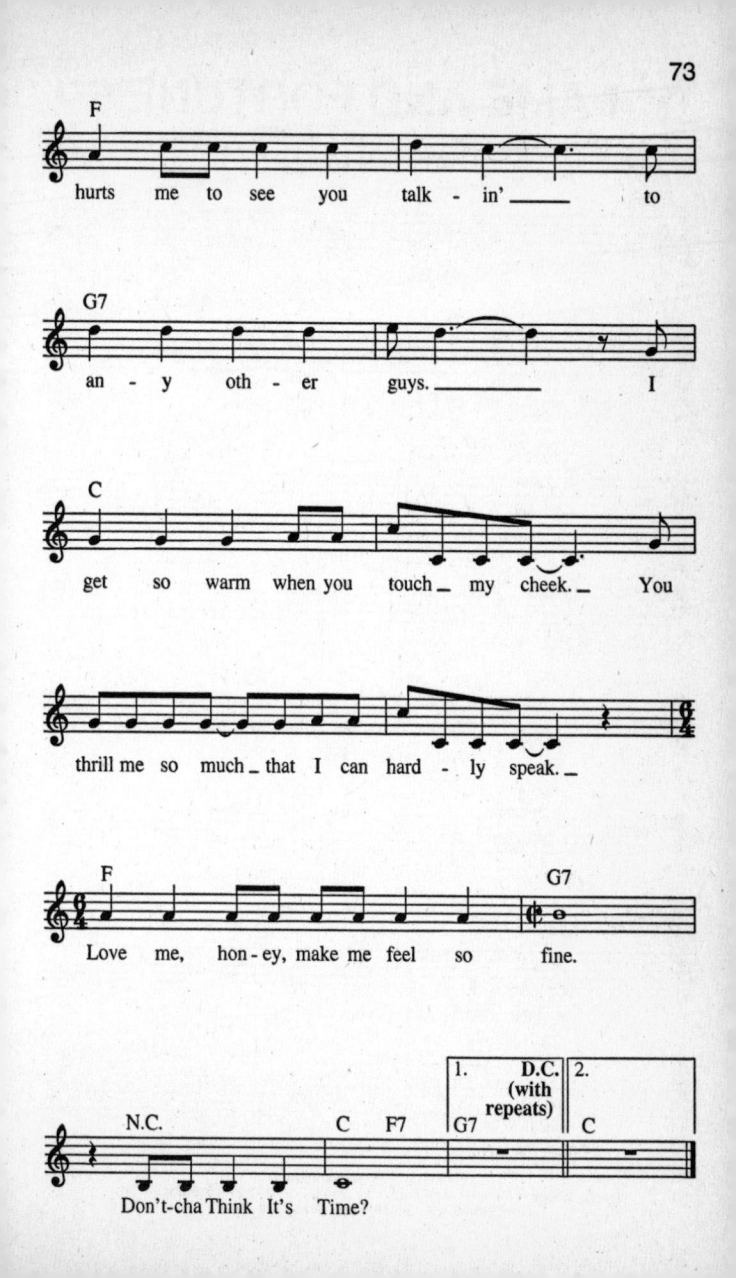
F
hurts me to see you talk - in' to
G7
an - y oth - er guys. I
C
get so warm when you touch my cheek. You
thrill me so much that I can hard - ly speak.
F
G7
Love me, hon - ey, make me feel so fine.
1. D.C. (with repeats)
2.
N.C.
C F7
G7
C
Don't-cha Think It's Time?

FAME AND FORTUNE

Words by FRED WISE
Music by BEN WEISMAN

Copyright © 1960 Gladys Music, Inc.
Copyright Renewed, Assigned to Chappell & Co. and Erika Publishing
International Copyright Secured All Rights Reserved

F
love is a treas - ure I
C
hold. It's so much
Am7 D7
great - er than sil - ver or
Dm7 G7 G7b9
gold. I know that
C Em F
I'd have noth - ing if you should go a -
C Dm7 Fm/Ab
way. But to know that you
C Am7 Dm7 G7
love me brings Fame And For - tune my
1. C G7b9
way.
2. C F7 C
way.

FLAMING STAR

Words by SID WAYNE
Music by SHERMAN EDWARDS

Copyright © 1961 by Gladys Music, Inc.
Copyright Renewed and Assigned to Holly Hill Music and Keith-Valerie Music
International Copyright Secured All Rights Reserved

Eb
Cm
Flam - ing Star, don't you shine on me. Flam - ing Star.
Eb
Flam - ing Star, keep be-hind - a me,
Cm
Fm
Flam - ing Star. There's a lot of liv - in' I've
got to do. Give me
time to make a few dreams come true,
1.,2.
Cm
Flam - ing Star.
3.
Cm
Flam - ing Star.

FOLLOW THAT DREAM

Words by FRED WISE
Music by BEN WEISMAN

Copyright © 1962 Gladys Music, Inc.
Copyright Renewed, Assigned to Chappell & Co. and Erika Publishing
International Copyright Secured All Rights Reserved

Ab
Eb Ab
that you can do.
are all a - bout.
Eb N.C. Ab
You've got - ta Fol - low That Dream wher -
I've got - ta Fol - low That Dream wher -
Bb7 Eb
ev - er that dream may lead.
ev - er that dream may lead.
Cm
You've got - ta Fol - low That Dream to
I've got - ta Fol - low That Dream to
1.
Ab Bb7 Eb Ab7
find the love you need.
find the love I
2.
Eb N.C Eb Ab7 Eb
Got - ta find me need.

FOOL

Words and Music by JAMES LAST
and CARL SIGMAN

Copyright © 1972 Happy Musikverlag GMBH
All Rights Administered by Chappell & Co.
International Copyright Secured All Rights Reserved

Dm/F
C/E
Fool, you could have made her love you.
Cm/E♭
G/D
Fool, you on - ly had to love her. But
To Coda
D
G
Em
now her love is gone. Gone now the love and
B/D♯
Dm6
laugh - ter see your - self the morn - ing
C
E♭
af - ter. Can't you see her eyes are
G/D
D
G
D.C. al Coda
mist - y as she said good - bye.
CODA
G
gone.

(Now and Then There's)

A FOOL SUCH AS I

Words and Music by
BILL TRADER

Moderately slow, with expression

© Copyright 1952 by MCA MUSIC PUBLISHING, A Division of MCA INC.
Copyright Renewed
International Copyright Secured All Rights Reserved

MCA music publishing

F
F♯dim7
then, there's A Fool Such As
C/G
F/A Fm6/A♭
C
C♯dim7
G/D
I am o - ver you. You taught me how to
D7
D♯dim7
Em C♯dim7 Dm
A7
Fm6/A♭ G7 N.C.
love, and now you say that we are through. I'm a
C
E7
F
fool, but I'll love you, dear, un - til the day I
C C7/B♭ F/A A♭7♯11
C
G♯dim7 Am
Dm7
G7
die. Now and then, there's A Fool Such As
1.
C
Dm G7 N.C.
2.
C F C
I.
Par - don
I.

FOR THE GOOD TIMES

Words and Music by
KRIS KRISTOFFERSON

Copyright © 1968 by Careers-BMG Music Publishing, Inc.
Copyright Renewed
International Copyright Secured All Rights Reserved

C7
up - on my pil - low,
hold your warm and ten - der
F
Gm7
C7
bod - y close to mine.
Hear the
F
Fmaj7
F7
whis - per of the rain - drops blow - ing
B♭
B♭m
soft a - gainst the win - dow
C7
Gm
and make be - lieve you love me
one more
C7sus
C7
1.
F
F6
time
For The Good Times.
Fmaj7
F6
2.
F
B♭6
F
I'll get a - Good Times.

G.I. BLUES

Words and Music by SID TEPPER
and ROY C. BENNETT

Moderately bright

C

They give us a room with a
get has - sen - fef - fer and
like to be he - roes, but
Frau - leins are pret - ty as

view of the beau - ti - ful Rhine.
black pump - er - nick - el for chow.
all that we do here is march.
flow'rs, but we can't make a pass.

C7 F

They give us a room with a
We get has - sen-fef - fer and
We'd like to be he - roes, but
The Frau - leins are pret - ty as

C

view of the beau - ti - ful Rhine.
black pump - er - nick - el for chow.
all that we do here is march.
flow'rs, but we can't make a pass.

G7

Gim-me a mud - dy old creek in
I'd blow my next month's pay for a
And they don't give the Pur - ple
'Cause they're all wear-in' signs say-in',

Copyright © 1960 by Gladys Music, Inc.
Copyright Renewed and Assigned to Gladys Music (Administered by Williamson Music)
International Copyright Secured All Rights Reserved

F7
C
Tex - as an - y old time.
slice of Tex - as cow.
Heart for a fall - en arch.
"Keepen Sie off___ the grass!"
I've got those
C
hup, two, three, four, oc - cu - pa - tion G. I.
C7
F
Blues.
From my G. I. hair to the
3
C
heels of my G. I. shoes.
And if I
G7 N.C.
F7 N.C.
F7
don't go state - side___ soon, I'm gon - na blow my
1.-3.
C F7 G7
4.
C F7 C
fuse.
We
We'd
The
fuse.

GIRLS! GIRLS! GIRLS!

Words and Music by JERRY LEIBER
and MIKE STOLLER

© 1961, 1962 (Renewed 1990, 1991) JERRY LEIBER MUSIC and MIKE STOLLER MUSIC
All Rights Reserved

Bb7
boy and I can't stop think - in' a - bout
Eb
Girls, Girls, Girls,
Ab7
Girls. And when I pick up a
Eb7
sand - wich to munch, a - crunch - y
crunch - et - y, a - crunch - et - y crunch,
Ab7
I nev - er ev - er get to fin - ish my lunch,
F7
be - cause there's al - ways bound to
Bb7
Eb
be a bunch of girls, in tight

sweat - ers, girls, in short dress - es,
a - walk-in' and a - wig - gl - in' by yay,
Eb7 Ab
yay, yay. Girls, out boat - in',
Eb
girls just a - float - in', so pret - ty,
Lord, I could cry. I'm just a
F7 Bb7
red blood - ed boy and I can't stop
Eb7
think - in' a - bout Girls, Girls,
1. 2.
Girls, Girls. Girls,
Girls.

GOOD LUCK CHARM

Words and Music by AARON SCHROEDER
and WALLY GOLD

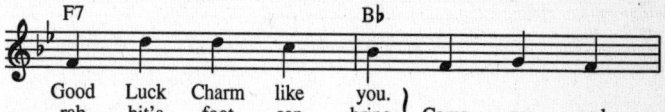

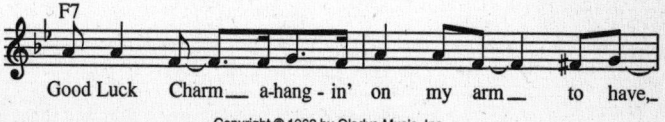

Copyright © 1962 by Gladys Music, Inc.
Copyright Renewed and Assigned to Gladys Music (Administered by Williamson Music)
and Rachel's Own Music (Administered by A. Schroeder International Ltd.)
International Copyright Secured All Rights Reserved

C7
F7
to have, to hold, to hold to - night.
1.
2.
B♭
To Coda
G♭9
F7
Uh-huh - huh,
C7
F7
uh-huh - huh,
uh-huh - huh;
B♭
oh, yeah.
Uh-huh - huh,
C7
F7
uh-huh - huh,
uh, to - night.

B♭
G♭9
F7
D.C. al Coda
CODA
C7
Uh-huh - huh,
uh-huh huh,
F7
B♭
uh-huh huh;
oh,
C7
yeah.
Uh-huh - huh,
uh-huh, - huh,
F7
B♭
E♭7
B♭
uh, to - night.

GOOD ROCKIN' TONIGHT

By ROY BROWN

Copyright © 1948 Blue Ridge Publishing Corporation
Copyright Renewed and Assigned to Fort Knox Music, Inc. and Trio Music Co., Inc.
International Copyright Secured All Rights Reserved
Used by Permission

there's Good Rock-in' To - night.

I say he'll meet me in a hur-ry, be -

hind the barn. Don't you be a-fraid, dar-lin', I'll

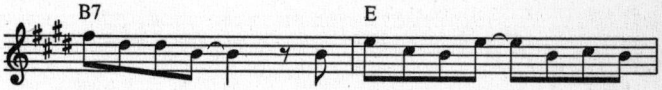

do you no harm. I want you to bring a-long my

rock-in' shoes 'cause to - night I'm gon-na rock a-way

all the blues. I heard the news:

there's Good Rock-in' To - night.

(Instrumental)
A7
E
B7
E7
Well, _ we gon-na rock.
A7
We gon-na rock. _
Let's rock,

E
B7
come on and rock.
We gon-na rock
all_

E
D.S. al Coda
_____ our blues a - way. _
Have you

CODA
Well,_ we're gon - na rock,
rock,

rock.
Ah, __ come on and rock,
rock,

A7
rock,
al-ways rock,
rock,
rock.
Ah,_ well let's

E
B
rock,
rock,
rock.
Ah,_ we gon-na rock
all_

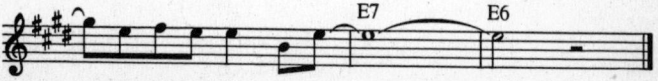
E7
E6
_____ our_ blues a - way. _____

GREEN GREEN GRASS OF HOME

Words and Music by
CURLY PUTMAN

Copyright © 1965 Sony/ATV Songs LLC
Copyright Renewed
All Rights Administered by Sony/ATV Music Publishing, 8 Music Square West, Nashville, TN 37203
International Copyright Secured All Rights Reserved

Bm Am G
lips like cher - ries. It's good to touch the
lips like cher - ries. It's good to touch the
walk at day - break. A - gain I'll touch the
D7 Am7 D7 G C G
Green, Green Grass Of Home. Yes, they'll
Green, Green Grass Of Home. Yes, they'll
Green, Green, Grass Of Home. Yes, they'll
G7
all come to meet me, arms
all come to meet me, arms
all come to see me in the
1., 2.
C Am7 G
reach - ing, smil-ing sweet - ly; It's good to touch the
reach - ing, smil-ing sweet - ly; It's good to touch the
D7 Am7 D7 G C G
Green, Green Grass Of Home. 2. The
Green, Green Grass Of Home. 3. (to recit.)
3.
C Bm Am G
shade of that old oak tree as they lay me 'neath the
D7 Am7 D7 C G/B Am7 G
Green, Green Grass Of Home.

HARD HEADED WOMAN

Words and Music by
CLAUDE DEMETRUIS

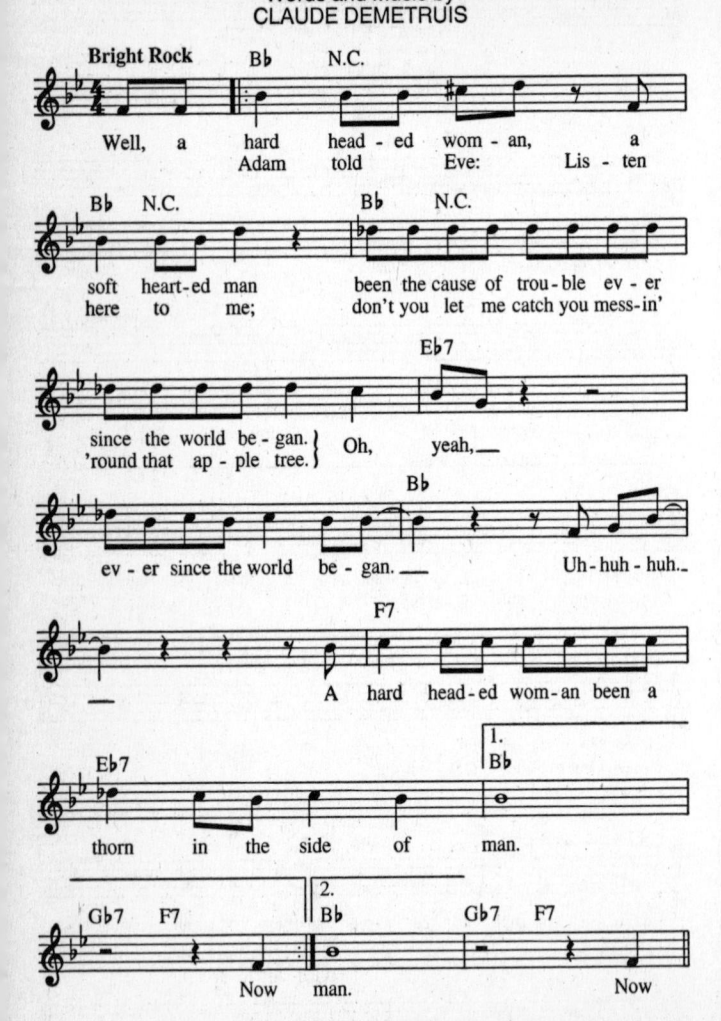

Copyright © 1958 by Gladys Music, Inc.
Copyright Renewed and Assigned to Gladys Music (Administered by Williamson Music)
International Copyright Secured All Rights Reserved

B♭ N.C. B♭ N.C.
Sam-son told De - li - lah loud and clear:
heard 'bout a king who was do - in' swell
I got a wom-an a head like a rock
B♭ N.C.
keep your cot - ton - pick - in' fin - gers
till he start - ed play - in' with that
if she ev - er went a - way I'd
E♭7
out my curl - y hair.
e - vil Jez - e - bel.
cry a - round the clock.
Oh, yeah,
B♭
ev-er since the world be-gan.
Uh-huh-huh.
A
F7 E♭7
Hard Head-ed Wom-an been a thorn in the side of
1.,2. 3.
B♭ G♭7 F7 B♭ E♭7 B♭
man. I man.

THE HAWAIIAN WEDDING SONG

(Ke Kali Nei Au)

English Lyrics by AL HOFFMAN and DICK MANNING
Hawaiian Lyrics and Music by CHARLES E. KING

Slowly, with much warmth

C G7 C C7 F G7 C G9
This is the mo - ment I've wait - ed for. I can
1. E - i - a - a - u ke ka - li nei A -
2. A he ha - li - a kai hi - ki mai No kuu

C G7 E7/G♯ Am Am/G D7/F♯ D7 G7
hear my heart sing - ing, soon bells will be ring - ing.
ia la i he - a ku - u a lo - ha
lei o - na - o - na pulu - pe - i ka u - a

C C/E E♭dim7 D7 G7 C/E
This is the mo - ment of sweet "A lo - ha,"
E - i - a a - u ke hu - li ne - i
Au - he - a o - e kai - ini a lo - ko

C G9
I will love you long - er than for - ev - er,
A lo - a - a o - e e ka i - po
Na lo - ko a - e ka ma - na o

G7 C G+
prom - ise me that you will leave me nev - er.
Ma - ha ka i - i - ni a ka pu - u - wai.
Hu - 'e la - ni a - na i kuu ki - no.

C A7 D7 G7
Here and now, dear, all my love I
U - a si - la pa - a ia me
Ku - u pu - a ku - u lei ona

© Copyright 1926, 1958 by CHARLES E. KING MUSIC CO.
Copyright Renewed 1986 and Assigned to CHARLES E. KING MUSIC CO., MCA MUSIC PUBLISHING,
A Division of MCA INC. and AL HOFFMANN SONGS, INC.
All Rights for CHARLES E. KING MUSIC CO. Controlled and Administered by MCA MUSIC PUBLISHING,
A Division of MCA INC.
International Copyright Secured All Rights Reserved

MCA music publishing

C
E♭dim7
vow, dear. Prom - ise me that you will leave me
o - e Ko a - lo - ha ma - ka - mae e
o - na A'u i kui a la - wa i - a -
G9
G7
nev - er, I will love you long - er than for -
i - po Ka - 'u ia e le - i a - e
ne - i Me ke a - la pu - a pi -
C
C7
ev - er. Now that we are
ne - i la Nou no ka i -
ka - ke A o oe kuu
F
D7
G7
one, clouds won't hide the sun. Blue
ini A nou wa - le no A
pua kuu pua lei le - hua A'u
C
A7
D7
G7
skies of Ha - wai - i smile on this, our wed - ding
o ko a - lo - ha ka'u e hi - i - po - i
e li - a ma - u nei hoo - paa ia iho kea -
C
A7
day. I do love you with
mau Na'u oe e lei na'u
loha He lei, oe na'u, he
D7
G7
1.
C
G7
2.
C
all my heart. heart.
oe e lei. lei.
lei oe na'u. na'u.

HEARTBREAK HOTEL

Words and Music by MAE BOREN AXTON,
TOMMY DURDEN and ELVIS PRESLEY

Copyright © 1956 Sony/ATV Songs LLC
Copyright Renewed
All Rights Administered by Sony/ATV Music Publishing, 8 Music Square West, Nashville, TN 37203
International Copyright Secured All Rights Reserved

E
die.
Al -
E
though it's al - ways crowd - ed,
Bell - hop's tears keep flow - ing,
still can find___some room, where those bro - ken
desk clerks dressed_ in black. They been so
heart - ed lov - ers cry a -
long on Lone - ly Street they ain't nev - er
A7
way their gloom, oh!
gonn' come back, oh!
I get so lone - ly,
B7
I get so lone - ly get so
E
D.C. and Fade
lone - ly I could die.

HELP ME MAKE IT THROUGH THE NIGHT

Words and Music by
KRIS KRISTOFFERSON

© 1970 TEMI COMBINE INC.
All Rights Controlled by COMBINE MUSIC CORP. and Administered by EMI BLACKWOOD MUSIC INC.
All Rights Reserved International Copyright Secured Used by Permission

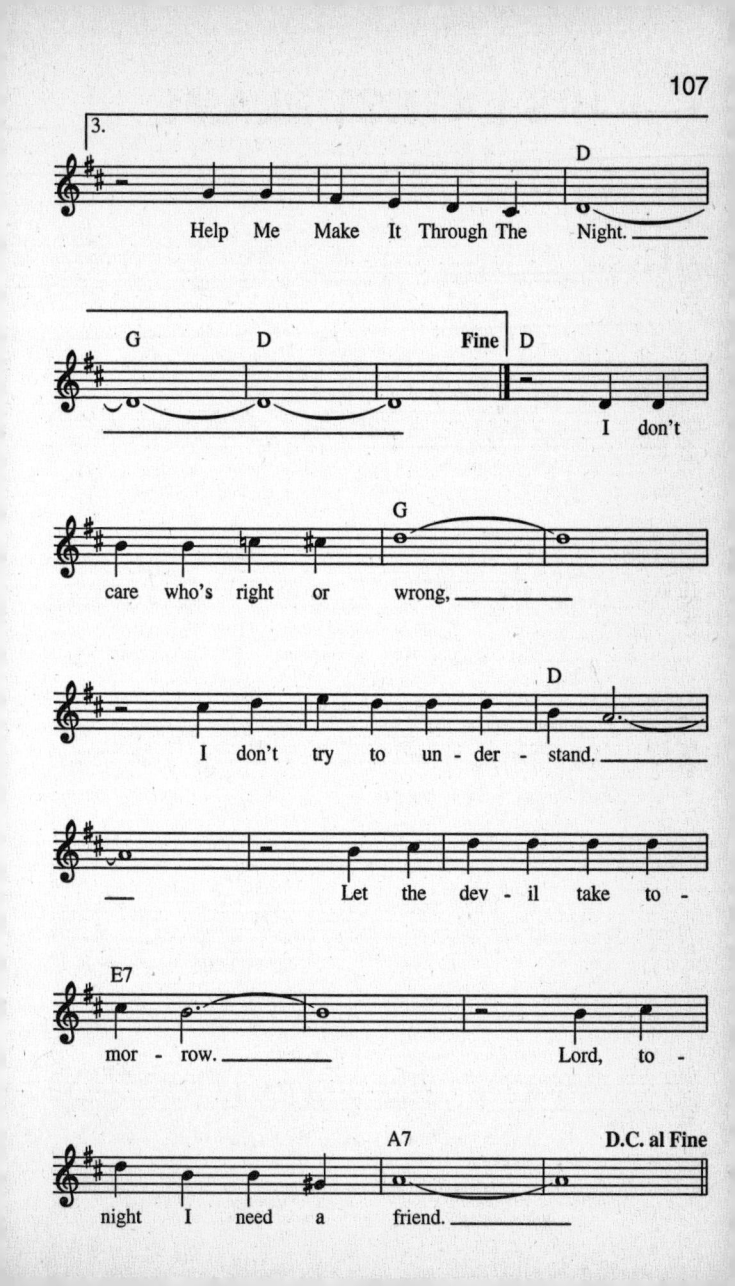
3.
D
Help Me Make It Through The Night.
G
D
Fine
D
I don't
G
care who's right or wrong,
D
I don't try to un - der - stand.
Let the dev - il take to -
E7
mor - row.
Lord, to -
A7
D.C. al Fine
night I need a friend.

HIS LATEST FLAME

Words and Music by DOC POMUS
and MORT SHUMAN

Copyright © 1961 by Valley Publishers, Inc.
Copyright Renewed and Assigned to Elvis Presley Music (Administered by R&H Music)
International Copyright Secured All Rights Reserved

C7 Bb C7
burn-in'. I wished him luck and
Bb C7 Bb
then he said good - bye.
C7 Bb C7
He was gone but still his words kept re - turn-in'.
Bb C7 Bb
What else was there for me to do but
F Dm F Dm N.C.
cry. Would you be -
F Dm F
lieve that yes - ter - day

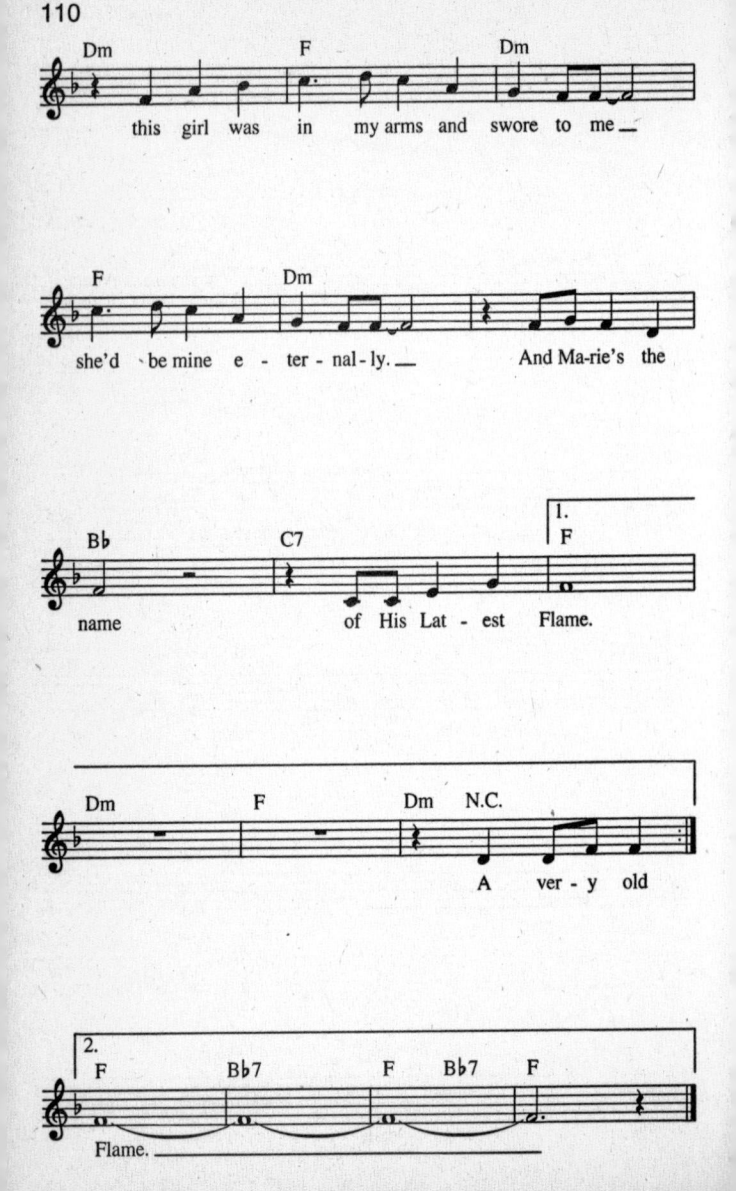
Dm
F
Dm
this girl was in my arms and swore to me
F
Dm
she'd be mine e - ter - nal - ly.
And Ma-rie's the
B♭
C7
1.
F
name
of His Lat - est Flame.
Dm
F
Dm
N.C.
A ver - y old
2.
F
B♭7
F
B♭7
F
Flame.

I FEEL SO BAD

Words and Music by
CHUCK WILLIS

Copyright © 1961 Tideland Music and Chuck Willis Music
Copyright Renewed 1989 Tideland Music and Chuck Willis Music
International Copyright Secured All Rights Reserved
Used by Permission

N.C.
F7
Shake my head and walk a - way.
(Instrumental)
Oo.
Peo - ple,
times I want to stay here,
then a -
that's the way I feel.
gain, I want to leave.
(Instrumental)
Bb7
Oo.
'Times I want to
leave here,
Peo - ple, that's the way I
then a - gain, I want to

F7
feel.
stay.
(Instrumental)
C7
Some - times I think I won't,
Yes, I got my train fare.
N.C.
then a - gain, I think I
Pack my grip and ride a -
F7
To Coda
will.
way.
(Instrumental)
D.S. al Coda
Some -
CODA
Repeat and Fade
(Instrumental)

HOUND DOG

Words and Music by JERRY LEIBER
and MIKE STOLLER

Copyright © 1956 by Elvis Presley Music, Inc. and Lion Publishing Co., Inc.
Copyright Renewed, Assigned to Gladys Music (Administered by Williamson Music)
and MCA Music Publishing, a Division of MCA Inc.
International Copyright Secured All Rights Reserved

N.C.
B♭
When they said you was high - classed,
well, that was just a lie.
E♭7
When they said you was high - classed,
B♭
well, that was just a lie.
F7
Well, you ain't nev - er caught a rab - bit and you
E♭7
1.
B♭
ain't no friend of mine.
N.C.
2.
B♭
E♭7
B♭
You ain't noth-in' but a mine.

I BEG OF YOU

Words and Music by ROSE MARIE McCOY
and KELLY OWENS

Copyright © 1957 by Rio Grande Music, Inc.
Copyright Assigned to Elvis Presley Music, Inc.
Copyright Renewed and Assigned to Elvis Presley Music (Administered by R&H Music)
International Copyright Secured All Rights Reserved

C
prom-ise that you'll al - ways love me true.
F7
Make me know you love me the
D7 N.C. G7sus
same way I love you, lit - tle girl. You
C
got me at your mer - cy now
C7
that I'm in love with you. So
F7
please don't take ad - van - tage 'cause you
C
know my love is true. My dar - ling,
G7 F7 C
please please love me too, I Beg Of You.
1.
A♭7 G7
I don't
2.
F7 C

I GOT STUNG

Words and Music by AARON SCHROEDER
and DAVID HILL

Copyright © 1958 by Gladys Music, Inc.
Copyright Renewed and Assigned to Gladys Music (Administered by Williamson Music)
and Rachel's Own Music (Administered by A. Schroeder International Ltd.)
International Copyright Secured All Rights Reserved

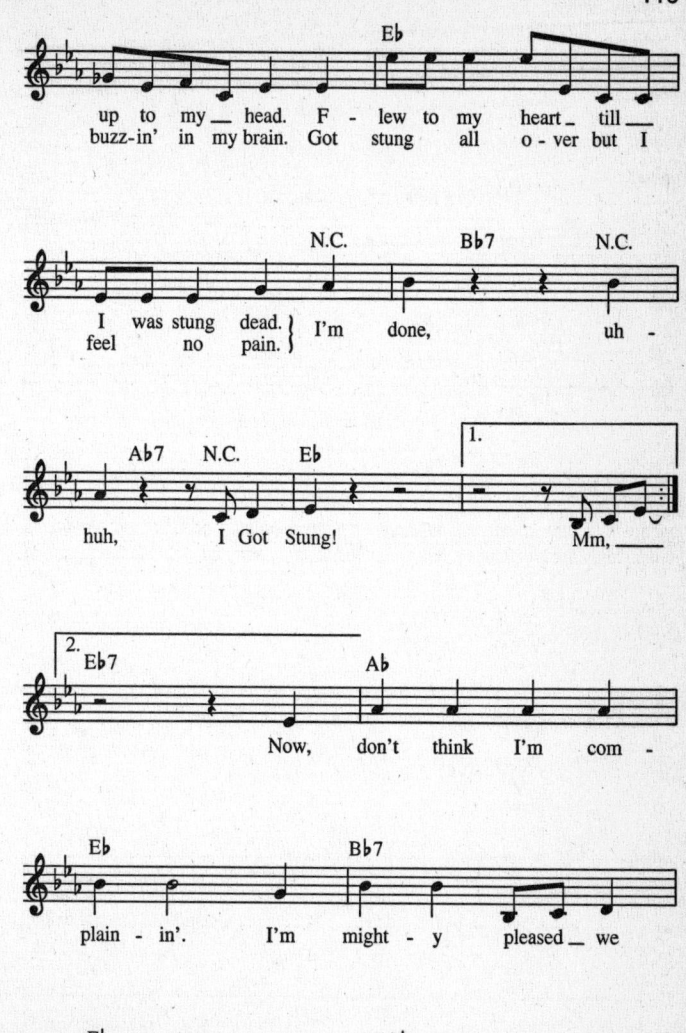
E♭
up to my head. F - lew to my heart till
buzz-in' in my brain. Got stung all o - ver but I
N.C.
B♭7
N.C.
I was stung dead.
feel no pain.
I'm done,
uh -
A♭7
N.C.
E♭
1.
huh,
I Got Stung!
Mm,
2.
E♭7
A♭
Now, don't think I'm com -
E♭
B♭7
plain - in'. I'm might - y pleased we
E♭
A♭
met, 'cause you gim-me just one lit - tle peck on the

Bb7 N.C.
back of my neck and I break out in a
Bb7 Eb
cold cold sweat. If I live to a hun - dred and
two, I won't let no - bod - y sting me but
Ab7
you. I'll be buzz - in' 'round your hive ev - 'ry
Eb
day at five, and I'm nev - er gon - na leave_ once
N.C. Bb7 N.C. Ab7 N.C.
I ar - rive 'cause I'm done, uh - huh, I Got
1.
Eb Ab7 Bb7 N.C.
Stung! Mm, Stung!
2.
Eb Ab7 Eb

IF I CAN DREAM

Words and Music by
W. EARL BROWN

Copyright © 1968 by Gladys Music, Inc.
Copyright Renewed and Assigned to Gladys Music (Administered by Williamson Music)
International Copyright Secured All Rights Reserved

2.
E♭7 Cm7 B♭ E♭/F B♭ E♭ B♭
why_ won't that sun ap - pear?
E♭ Edim B♭ B♭7
We're lost in a cloud_ with too much rain.
E♭ Edim
We're trapped in a world
B♭ B♭7
that's trou - bled with pain.
E♭ Edim
But as long as a man has the
B♭/F D7 Gm C9
strength to dream, he can re - deem his soul and
Cm7/F Fm7 F7 G G7
fly. He can fly. Deep in my
C Am F6 G7
heart there's a trem - blin' ques - tion, still I am

C Em Am Em
sure that the an - swer's gon - na
Dm G7 F/G C C7
come some-how. Out there in the dark there's a beck-on-ing
F7 F♯dim
can - dle, and while I can
C Am
think, while I can talk, while I can
C Am
stand, while I can walk, while I can
Fmaj7 Dm7
dream, please let my dream come
Dm7/G G7 C Am
true right now!
C Am C F C

I GOTTA KNOW

Words and Music by PAUL EVANS
and MATT WILLIAMS

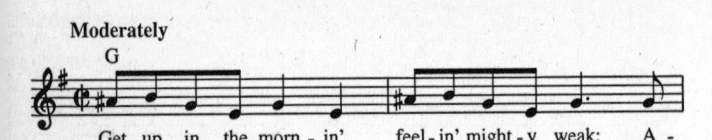

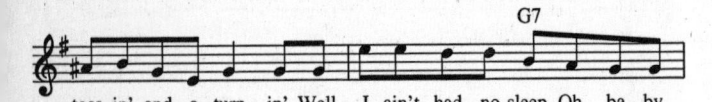

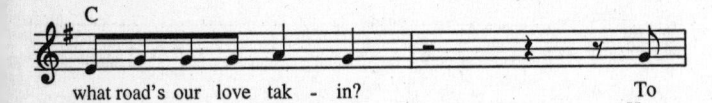

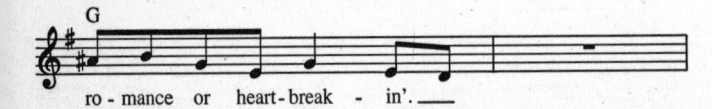

Copyright © 1959 by Gladys Music, Inc.
Copyright Renewed and Assigned to Gladys Music (Administered by Williamson Music) and Port Music, Inc.
International Copyright Secured All Rights Reserved

D7
N.C.
Won't you say which way you're gon - na go.
Tell me if you love me, yes or no.
Will you kiss a - way my cares and woe?
I got - ta
To Coda
G
C
1.
G
know, got - ta know, got - ta know.
2.
G
C
D7
know. Oh, how much I
G
C
D7
need you! Have pit - y on this heart of
G
C
D7
mine. Well, if you need and
G
Em
A7 N.C.
want me too, I'll be your one and on - ly till the
D7
D.C. al Coda
end of time.
CODA
G
know.

I NEED YOUR LOVE TONIGHT

Words and Music by SID WAYNE
and BIX REICHNER

Copyright © 1959 by Gladys Music, Inc.
Copyright Renewed and Assigned to Gladys Music (Administered by Williamson Music) and Holly Hill Music
International Copyright Secured All Rights Reserved

B♭ F
I've been wait - in' just for to - night to
C7 F
do some lov - in' and hold you tight. Don't
B♭ F
tell me, ba - by, you got - ta go; I got the
G7 N.C. C7 N.C.
hi - fi high and the lights down low. Hey,
F C7
now, hear what I say. Ooh -
F
wow, you bet - ter stay. Pow -
F7 B♭
pow, don't run a - way. I
1. 2.
F C7 F C7 N.C.
Need Your Love To - night. Oh,

I WANT YOU, I NEED YOU, I LOVE YOU

Words by MAURICE MYSELS
Music by IRA KOSLOFF

Copyright © 1956 by Elvis Presley Music, Inc.
Copyright Renewed and Assigned to Gladys Music (Administered by Williamson Music)
International Copyright Secured All Rights Reserved

F C E7
for. I Want You, I Need You, I
A7 Dm7 G7
Love You more and
C Gm7 C7
more. I thought I could live with-out
F Gm7 C7
ro - mance be - fore you came to
F Am7 D7 G Em
me, but now I know that I will go on
Am7 D7 G7sus G7
lov - ing you e - ter - nal - ly. Won't you
C Am Dm G7
please be my own? Nev-er leave me a - lone, 'Cause I
C C7 F
die ev - 'ry time we're a - part. I
C E7 A7
Want You, I Need You, I Love You with
Dm7 G7
all my heart.
1. C A♭7 G7 N.C.
2. C
Hold me heart.

I WAS THE ONE

Words and Music by CLAUDE DEMETRUIS,
BILL PEPPERS, HAL BLAIR and AARON SCHROEDER

Copyright © 1956 by Chappell & Co., and Rachel's Own Music
(Administered by A. Schroeder International Ltd.)
Copyright Renewed
International Copyright Secured All Rights Reserved

C Dm7/G G7 C C7
I taught (her) (him) so well. And
F Fm
then one day I had my love as
C G7♯5 C
per - fect as could be. (She) (He)
D7
lived, (she) (he) loved, (she) (he) laughed, (she) (he) cried;
A♭7♯11 G7
and it was all for me. But
C Am Dm7 G7♭9
I'll nev-er know who taught (her) (him) to lie, and
C Am Dm7 G7
now that it's o - ver and done,
C C7 F Fm
who learned the les - son when (she) (he) broke my heart?
C Dm7 G7
1. C A♭7 G7
2. C F7 C
I Was The One. One.

I'M LEAVIN'

Words and Music by
MICHAEL JARRETT and SONNY CHARLES

Copyright © 1971 by Elvis Presley Music (Administered by R&H Music)
International Copyright Secured All Rights Reserved

A7
Tried so hard each time, each time
I just can't make it.
Feel - in' fast vi - bra - tions, and
I just can't take it.
Gm
Liv - in' from day to day,
Dmaj7
chas - in' a dream.
Em F♯m G A
I'm,
Em F♯m G A
I'm
A7 D
Repeat and Fade
Leav - in'.

I'M SO LONESOME I COULD CRY

Words and Music by
HANK WILLIAMS

Copyright © 1949 by Hiriam Music and Acuff-Rose Music, Inc. in the U.S.A.
Copyright Renewed
All Rights for Hiriam Music Administered by Rightsong Music Inc.
All Rights outside the U.S.A. Controlled by Acuff-Rose Music, Inc.
International Copyright Secured All Rights Reserved

nev - er seen a
si - lence of a
night so long when
fall - ing star lights
time goes crawl - ing
up a pur - ple
F7
B♭
by. The moon just
sky. And as I
F
went be - hind a
won - der where you
cloud to hide its
are, I'm So Lone - some
C7
1.
F
face and cry.
I Could
(D.C.)
2.
F
Did you Cry.

I'VE GOT A THING ABOUT YOU, BABY

Words and Music by
TONY JOE WHITE

© 1972, 1974 TENNESSEE SWAMP FOX MUSIC CO.
All Rights Controlled and Administered by EMI APRIL MUSIC INC.
All Rights Reserved International Copyright Secured Used by Permission

gon - na be here to do.
drive you out of your mind.
I Got A
F
Em
Thing A - bout You, Ba - by; ain't
Dm
C
noth - ing I can do.
I Got A
F
Em
Thing A - bout You, Ba - by, a
Dm
To Coda
1.
C
thing a - bout a - lov - in' you.
(Instrumental)
2.
C
D.S. al Coda
I Got A
CODA
C

I'VE LOST YOU

Words and Music by
KEN HOWARD and ALAN BLAIKLEY

Copyright © 1970 by Carlin Music Corp. (Administered by Gladys Music c/o Williamson Music)
International Copyright Secured All Rights Reserved

F7sus
F7
mind. Oh, I've
know. Oh, I've
well. Oh, I've
𝄋
B♭
Lost You, though you're near me and your
Lost You, yes, I've Lost You, I can't
Lost You, oh, I've Lost You, though you
B♭7
bod - y's still as kind. I've
reach you an - y - more. We
won't ad - mit it's so. I've
E♭
Lost You on the jour - ney, but I
ought to talk it o - ver now, but
Lost You on the jour - ney, but I
1., 2.
F7
(D.C.)
can't re - mem - ber where or when.
rea - son can't stand in for feel - ing.
3.
F7
can't re - mem - ber where or when.
B♭
F/A
Gm
Dm
(Instrumental)
D.S. (Lyric 1) and Fade
E♭
B♭/D
F7sus
F7
Oh, I've

IF YOU TALK IN YOUR SLEEP

Words and Music by
BOBBY "RED" WEST and JOHNNY CHRISTOPHER

Moderately slow (in 2)

Copyright © 1974 Easy Nine Music (administered by Copyright Management, Inc.),
Elvis Presley Music and Herb O'Mell Music
International Copyright Secured All Rights Reserved
Used by Permission

G5
G7sus
Em
And if you walk in your sleep,
To Coda
1.
C
D
G5
G7sus
for-get where you came.
(Instrumental)
G5
G7sus
G5
G7sus
2.
G5
G7sus
(Instrumental)
G5
G7sus
G5
G7sus
G5
G7sus
G5
G7sus
D.S. al Coda
CODA
G5
G7sus
For-get where you came
G5
G7sus
Repeat and Fade
now.
Don't men-tion my name.

IN THE GHETTO
(The Vicious Circle)

Words and Music by
MAC DAVIS

© 1969 SCREEN GEMS-EMI MUSIC INC. and ELVIS PRESLEY MUSIC, INC.
All Rights Controlled and Administered by SCREEN GEMS-EMI MUSIC INC.
All Rights Reserved International Copyright Secured Used by Permission

D A D E
help - ing hand or he'll grow to be an an-gry young man
A E
some day. Take a look at you and me; are we too
D A D C#m
blind to see or do we sim - ply turn our heads
Bm E A D A
and look the oth-er way? Well, the world turns,
D A C#m
and a hun-gry lit-tle boy with a run - ny nose
D E A D A
plays in the street as the cold wind blows In The Ghet-to.
D A D A
And his hun-ger burns.
D A C#m
So he starts to roam the streets at night, and he
D E
learns how to steal and he learns how to fight In The

A D A D A E
Ghet-to. And then one night in des-per-a - tion, a
D A D C♯m
young man breaks a - way. He buys a gun, steals a car,
Bm E A D A
tries to run but he don't get far. And his ma-ma cries
D A C♯m
as a crowd gath-ers 'round an an - gry young man face
D E
down in the street with a gun in his hand In The
A D A D A
Ghet - to. As her
D A C♯m
young man dies on a cold and grey Chi-ca - go morn - in', an-
D E A D A
oth-er lit-tle ba - by child is born In The Ghet - to.
D A D A
And his ma-ma cries.

KENTUCKY RAIN

Words and Music by
EDDIE RABBITT and DICK HEARD

Copyright © 1970 by Elvis Presley Music, Inc. and S-P-R Music Corp.
Copyright Assigned to Elvis Presley Music and Careers-BMG Music Publishing, Inc.
All Rights Administered by R&H Music
International Copyright Secured All Rights Reserved

C G
So I'm walk - ing in the rain,
Fi - n'lly got a ride with a
C F C F
thumb-ing for a ride on this lone - ly Ken-tuck-y
preach-er man who asked, "Where you bound on such a dark aft-er-
C C7 F G
back road. I've loved you much too long and
noon?" As we drove on through the rain, as he
C Am D7
my love's too strong to let you go, nev - er
lis - tened, I ex-plained, and he left me with a
G7 Fmaj7
know - ing what went wrong.
prayer that I'd find you.
D7 C Bm
Ken - tuck - y Rain keeps pour - ing down,
Em Am G F Em
and up a - head's an - oth - er town that I'll go

PROPERTY OF
HIGH POINT PUBLIC LIBRARY
HIGH POINT, NORTH CAROLINA

IT HURTS ME

Words and Music by
JOY BYERS and CHARLES E. DANIELS

Copyright © 1964 by Elvis Presley Music, Inc.
Copyright Renewed and Assigned to Elvis Presley Music (Administered by R&H Music)
International Copyright Secured All Rights Reserved

F Bb Bb7 Eb
way he makes you cry. You love him so
F Bb Gm
much you're too blind to see
Eb F Bb Bb7
he's on - ly play-ing a game.
Eb Edim Bb/F D7/F#
He nev - er loved you; he nev - er
Gm C
will. And, dar - ling, don't you know he'll nev - er
CODA
F D.S. al Coda Gm
change? you.
Bb Gm
Wait - ing to hold you so tight,
Bb Gm Eb
wait-ing to kiss you to - night, yes, dar-ling, to
Freely
F N.C. Cm7 Bb/D Cm7 Bb
find some-one like you.

IT'S NOW OR NEVER

Words and Music by
AARON SCHROEDER and WALLY GOLD

Copyright (for the U.S.A.) © 1960 by Gladys Music, Inc.
U.S.A. Copyright Renewed and Assigned to Gladys Music (Administered by Williamson Music) and Rachel's Own Music (Administered by A.Schroeder International Ltd.);
rights for all countries in the world (except U.S.A.) owned by Edizioni Bideri S.p.A, Naples
International Copyright Secured All Rights Reserved

Eb+ Ab
with your smile so ten - der,
we would cry an o - cean
Bb7
my heart was cap - tured, my soul sur -
if we lost true love and sweet de -
Eb N.C. Eb
ren - dered. I've spent a life - time
vo - tion. Your lips ex - cite me;
Eb+ Ab
wait - ing for the right time.
let your arms in - vite me,
Abm Eb F#dim
Now that you're near the time is
for who knows when we'll meet a -
Fm7 Bb7
1.
Eb Abm Eb N.C.
here at last. It's Now Or
gain this
2.
Eb Abm Eb N.C.
D.S. al Coda
way. It's Now Or
CODA
Bb7 Eb
my love won't wait.

JAILHOUSE ROCK

Words and Music by
JERRY LEIBER and MIKE STOLLER

© 1957 (Renewed) JERRY LEIBER MUSIC and MIKE STOLLER MUSIC
All Rights Reserved

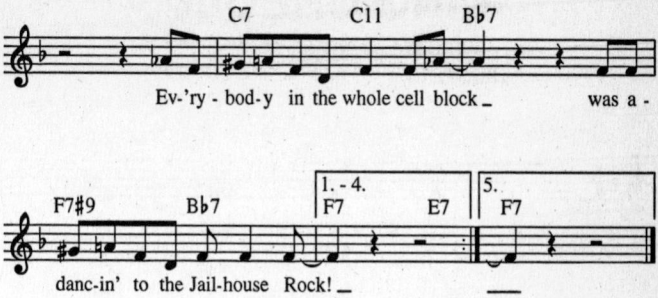

Additional Lyrics

4. The sad sack was a-sittin' on a block of stone,
   Way over in the corner weeping all alone.
   The warden said, "Hey, buddy, don't you be no square.
   If you can't find a partner, use a wooden chair!"
   Let's rock, *etc.*

5. Shifty Henry said to Bugs, "For Heaven's sake,
   No one's lookin'; now's our chance to make a break."
   Bugsy turned to Shifty and he said, "Nix, nix;
   I wanna stick around a while and get my kicks."
   Let's rock, *etc.*

KING CREOLE

Words and Music by
JERRY LEIBER and MIKE STOLLER

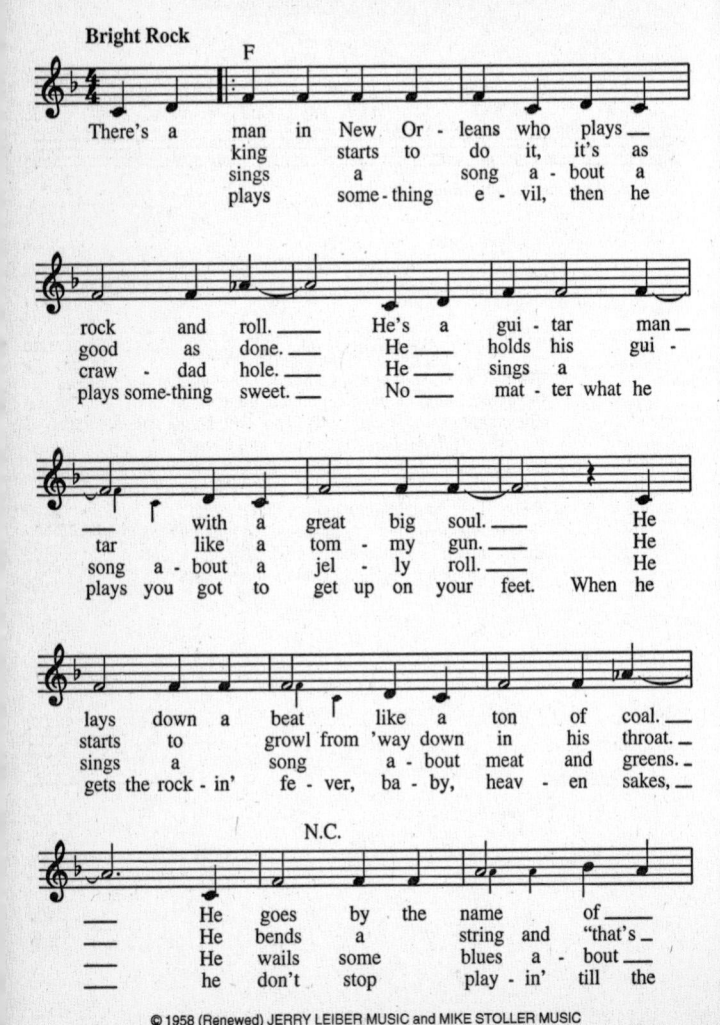

© 1958 (Renewed) JERRY LEIBER MUSIC and MIKE STOLLER MUSIC
All Rights Reserved

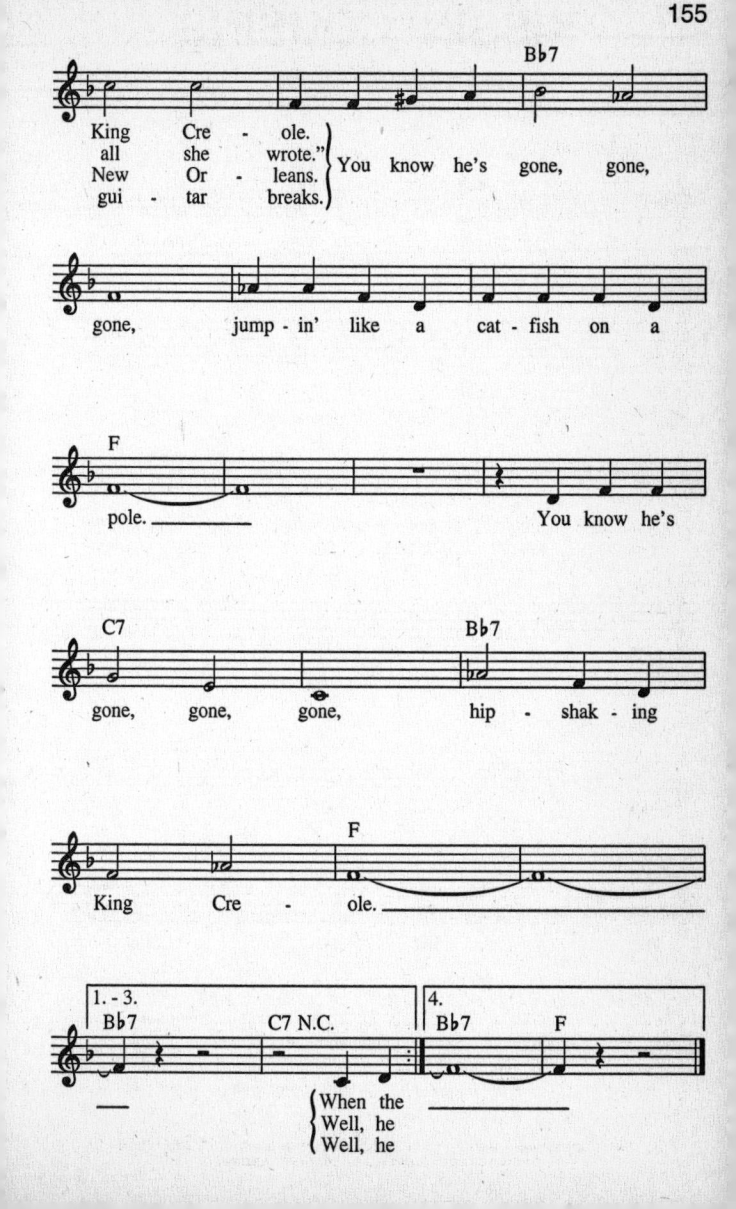
Bb7
King Cre - ole.
all she wrote."
New Or - leans.
gui - tar breaks.
You know he's gone, gone,
gone, jump - in' like a cat - fish on a
F
pole.
You know he's
C7
Bb7
gone, gone, gone, hip - shak - ing
F
King Cre - ole.
1. - 3.
Bb7
C7 N.C.
4.
Bb7
F
When the
Well, he
Well, he

KISSIN' COUSINS

Words and Music by
FRED WISE and RANDY STARR

Copyright © 1964 by Gladys Music
Copyright Renewed, Assigned to Erika Publishing and Nadel Music for the United States
International Copyright Secured All Rights Reserved

1.
F
— all right, all right, all right. Oh,
2.
F
— all right, all right, all right.
B♭
F
Yeah, we're all cous - ins,
B♭
3
F
that's what I be - lieve;
B♭
F
be - cause we're
'cause we're all
chil - dren
G7
C7
of Ad - am and Eve! Now
F
B♭7
I got a gal, and she wants a — lot of love.
F
— That's the
B♭7
kind of trou - ble I need — plen - ty

F
of.
We'll
B♭7
F
kiss
all
night,
I'll
B♭7
F
squeeze
her
tight.
We'll be
C7
B♭7
Kiss-in' Cous - ins, and that-'ll make it all right,
1.
F
all right, all right, all right.
2.
F
all right, all right, all right. We'll be
C7
B♭7
Kiss-in' Cous - ins, and that-'ll make it all right,
F
Repeat ad lib. and Fade
all right, all right, all right. We'll be

LITTLE SISTER

Words and Music by
DOC POMUS and MORT SHUMAN

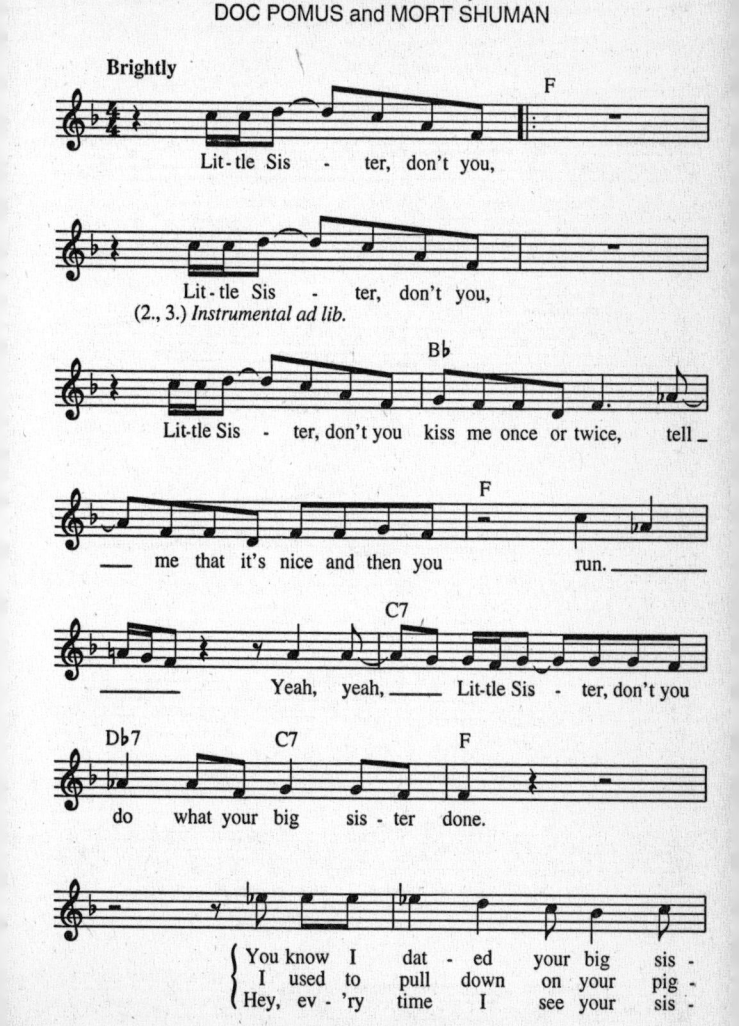

Copyright © 1961 by Elvis Presley Music, Inc.
Copyright Renewed and Assigned to Elvis Presley Music (Administered by R&H Music)
International Copyright Secured All Rights Reserved

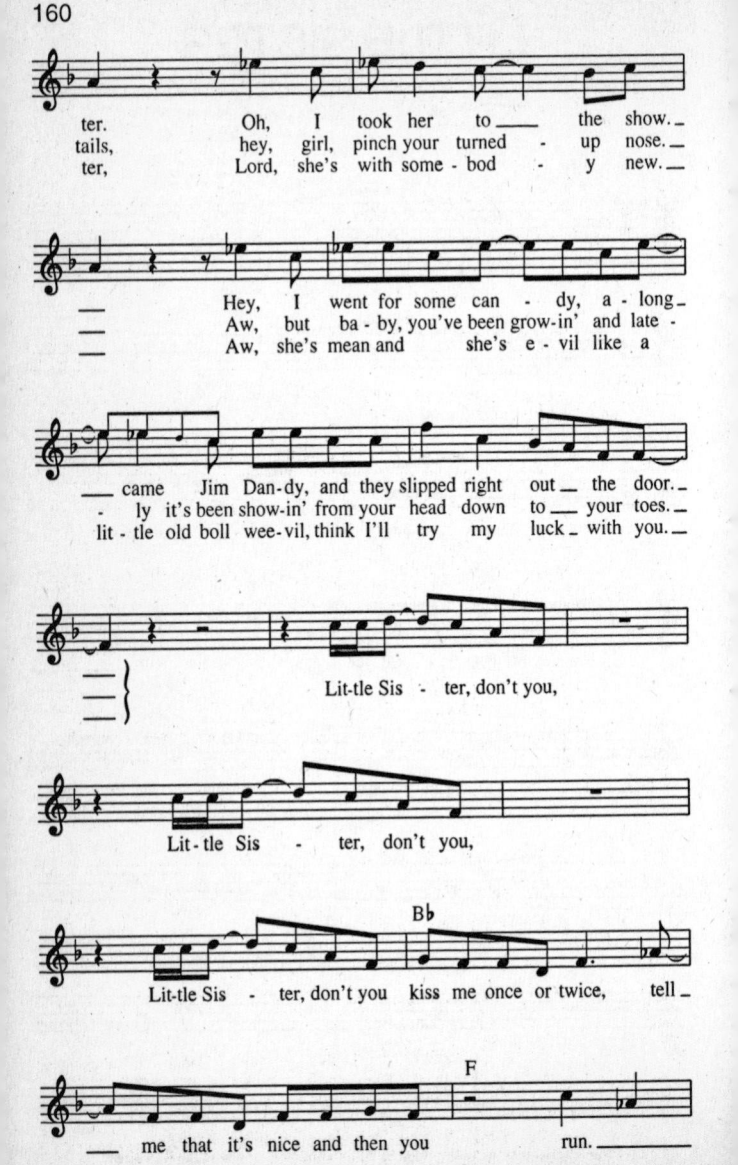
ter. Oh, I took her to the show.
tails, hey, girl, pinch your turned - up nose.
ter, Lord, she's with some - bod - y new.
Hey, I went for some can - dy, a - long
Aw, but ba - by, you've been grow-in' and late -
Aw, she's mean and she's e - vil like a
came Jim Dan-dy, and they slipped right out the door.
- ly it's been show-in' from your head down to your toes.
lit - tle old boll wee-vil, think I'll try my luck with you.
Lit-tle Sis - ter, don't you,
Lit - tle Sis - ter, don't you,
B♭
Lit-tle Sis - ter, don't you kiss me once or twice, tell
F
me that it's nice and then you run.

C7
Yeah, Lit-tle Sis - ter, don't you
Db7
C7
1., 2.
F
do what your big sis - ter done. Huh! Huh!
Huh! Huh!
3.
F
done.
C7
Well, Lit-tle Sis - ter, don't you
Db7
C7
F
do what your big sis - ter done.
C7
Ah, Lit-tle Sis - ter, don't you
Db7
C7
F
do what your big sis - ter done.

LONELY MAN

Words and Music by
BENNIE BENJAMIN and SOL MARCUS

Copyright © 1961 by Gladys Music
Copyright Renewed and Assigned to Bennie Benjamin Music, Inc. and WB Music Corp.
All Rights for Bennie Benjamin Music, Inc. Administered by Chappell & Co.
All Rights for the world excluding the United States Controlled
by Gladys Music (Administered by Williamson Music)
International Copyright Secured All Rights Reserved

Eb
Ab
Bb7
Lone - ly Man who trav - els all a -
Eb
Bb7
Eb
lone. When he has no one
Ab
Eb
Bb7
that he can call his own.
Ab
Al - ways so un - hap - py, tak - in'
Eb
F#dim
Eb
shel - ter where he can. Here I
Bb7
3
am; come meet a lone - ly, Lone - ly
1.
Eb Ab7 Bb7 N.C.
2.
Eb Ab7 Eb
Man. It's a Man.

LOVE ME

Words and Music by
JERRY LEIBER and MIKE STOLLER

© 1954 (Renewed) JERRY LEIBER MUSIC and MIKE STOLLER MUSIC
All Rights Reserved

G
C
you, dear, on - ly.
G
N.C.
C
I would beg and steal
G
just to feel your
A7
heart beat - ing close to
D7
A7
D7
N.C.
mine. Ev - 'ry night I
G
3
G7
pray to the stars that shine a -
C
bove me. Beg - ging on my
D7
knees, all I ask is please, please,
G
C7
1.
G
2.
G
Love Me. Treat me like a

LOVING YOU

Words and Music by
JERRY LEIBER and MIKE STOLLER

© 1957 (Renewed) JERRY LEIBER MUSIC and MIKE STOLLER MUSIC
All Rights Reserved

F
If I'm seen with some - one new,
C7
don't be blue, don't be blue.
I'll be faith - ful, I'll be true,
F
F7
al - ways true, true to you.
B♭
There is on - ly one for me, and
F
Cm6
D7
G7
you know who. You know that I'll
1.
C7
al - ways be Lov - ing
F
Bdim7
C7
(D.C.)
2.
C7
F
You. Lov - ing You.

MARY IN THE MORNING

Words and Music by
JOHNNY CYMBAL and MIKE LENDELL

© Copyright 1967 by DUCHESS MUSIC CORPORATION, an MCA company
Copyright Renewed
International Copyright Secured All Rights Reserved
MCA music publishing

F
D7
sun - light shin - ing on her gold - en
Ma - ry wakes to love an - oth - er
mor - rows for a life - time we will
To Coda
G7
C
hair.
day.
share.
Am
When I a - wake and see her
And Ma - ry's there in sun - ny
G
there so close be - side me,
days or storm - y weath - er.
Am
F
I want to take her in my
She does - n't care 'cause right or
D7
arms; the ache is there so deep in -
wrong, the love we share we share to -
1.
G7
(D.C.)
2.
G7
D.C. al Coda
side me.
geth - er.
CODA
C
F
C
Repeat and Fade
(Instrumental)

MEAN WOMAN BLUES

Words and Music by
CLAUDE DEMETRUIS

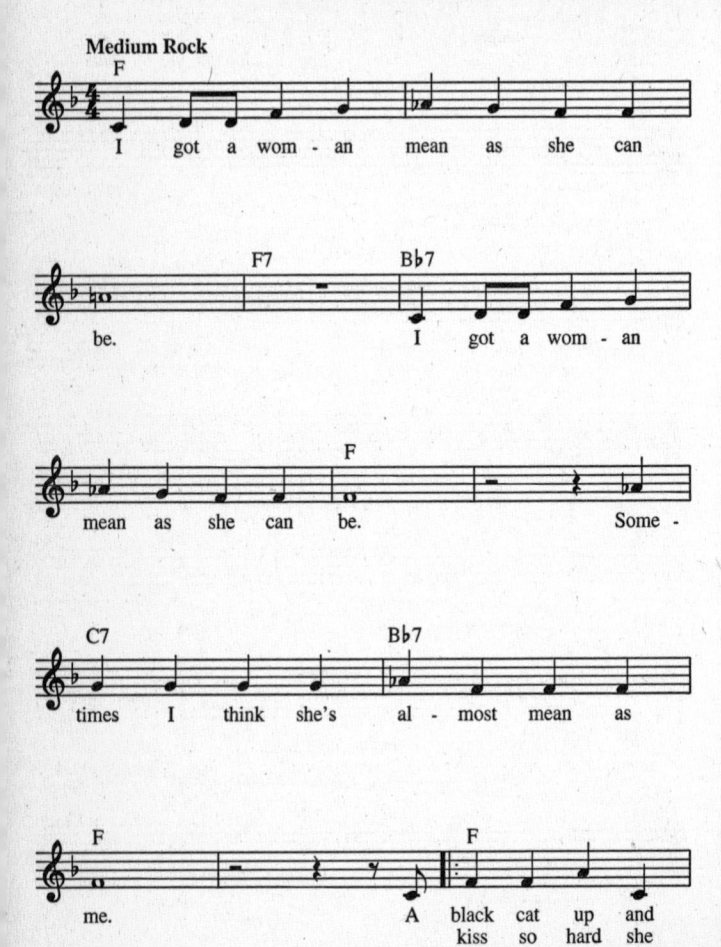

Copyright © 1957 by Gladys Music, Inc.
Copyright Renewed and Assigned to Gladys Music (Administered by Williamson Music)
International Copyright Secured All Rights Reserved

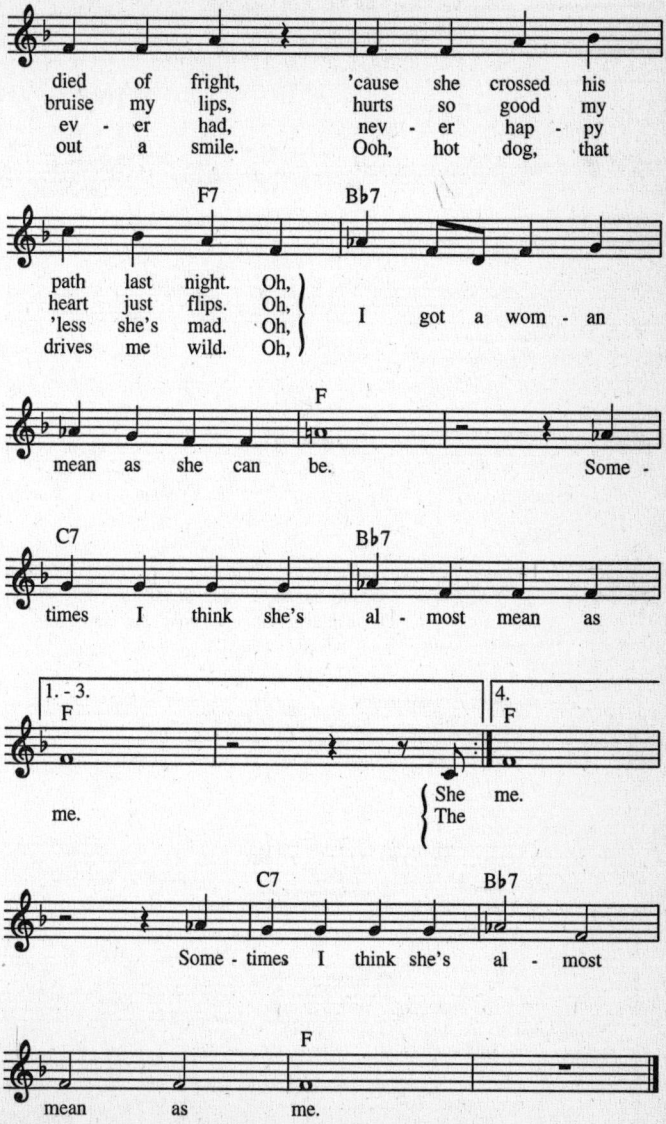
died of fright, 'cause she crossed his
bruise my lips, hurts so good my
ev - er had, nev - er hap - py
out a smile. Ooh, hot dog, that
F7
Bb7
path last night. Oh,
heart just flips. Oh,
'less she's mad. Oh,
drives me wild. Oh,
I got a wom - an
F
mean as she can be.
Some -
C7
Bb7
times I think she's al - most mean as
1. - 3.
F
me.
4.
F
She me.
The
C7
Bb7
Some - times I think she's al - most
F
mean as me.

MEMORIES

Words and Music by
BILLY STRANGE and SCOTT DAVIS

Copyright © 1969 by Gladys Music, Inc.
Copyright Assigned to Gladys Music (Administered by Williamson Music)
International Copyright Secured All Rights Reserved

Bbmaj7
Ebmaj7
Bbmaj7
ries.
Sweet Mem - o - ries
Ebmaj7
Bb
of hold - ing hands and red bou - quets and
Bb6
twi - light trimmed in pur - ple haze and
Ebdim
laugh - ing eyes and sim - ple ways and
Eb6
Ebdim
Bb
Bbsus
qui - et nights and gen - tle days with you.
Bbmaj7
Eb
Mem - o - ries pressed be - tween the pag - es of my
Bbmaj7
Ebmaj7
Bbmaj7
mind.
Mem - o - ries,
Eb
Bbmaj7
sweet - ened through the ag - es just like wine.
Repeat ad lib. and Fade
Bbsus
Bbmaj7
Bbsus
Mem - o - ries,
Mem - o -

A MESS OF BLUES

Words and Music by
DOC POMUS and MORT SHUMAN

Copyright © 1960 by Elvis Presley Music, Inc.
Copyright Renewed and Assigned to Elvis Presley Music (Administered by R&H Music)
International Copyright Secured All Rights Reserved

C B7 C7
tear - drop, roll - in' down my face.
F7
If you cry when you're in love, it
G7 N.C.
sure ain't no dis - grace. I got - ta
C
get my - self to - geth - er be -
fore I lose my mind. I'm gon - na
F7
catch the next train go - in' and
leave my blues be - hind. Since you're
G7 F7 C F7 C
gone I got A Mess Of Blues.

MY BABY LEFT ME

Words and Music by
ARTHUR CRUDUP

Copyright © 1956 by Elvis Presley Music, Inc.
Copyright Renewed and Assigned to Elvis Presley Music (Administered by R&H Music)
International Copyright Secured All Rights Reserved

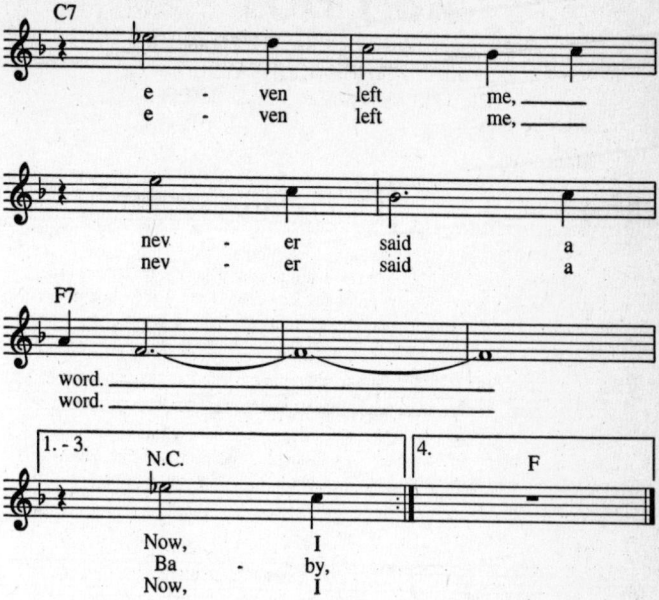

Additional Lyrics

3. Baby, one of these mornings, Lord, it won't be long,
   You'll look for me and, baby, and Daddy he'll be gone.
   You know you left me, you know you left me.
   My baby even left me, never said goodbye.

4. Now, I stand at my window, wring my hands and moan.
   All I know is that the one I love is gone.
   My Baby Left Me, you know she left me.
   My baby even left me, never said a word.

MY BOY

Words and Music by CLAUDE FRANCOIS,
JEAN-PIERRE BOURTAYRE,
BILL MARTIN and PHIL COULTER

© 1971, 1972 EMI MUSIC PUBLISHING LTD.
All Rights for the U.S.A. and Canada Controlled and Administered by COLGEMS-EMI MUSIC INC.
All Rights Reserved International Copyright Secured Used by Permission

F♯
F♯7
Bm
tried.
same.
grow.
Be - cause you're all I have, My
Em7
3
A7/C♯
A
Boy. You are my life, my pride, my
D
Bm/G♯
joy. And if I stay, I stay be -
C♯7♭9
F♯(add9)
1., 2.
F♯
(D.C.)
cause of you, My Boy.
3.
F♯7
Bm
Be - cause you're all I have, My
Em7
3
A7/C♯
Boy. You are my life, my pride, my
D
Bm/G♯
joy. And if I stay, I stay be -
C♯7♭9
F♯(add9)
F♯7
Repeat and Fade
cause of you, My Boy. Be - cause you're

MY WAY

English Words by PAUL ANKA
Original French Words by GILES THIBAULT
Music by JACQUES REVAUX and CLAUDE FRANCOIS

Moderately slow

Copyright © 1967 Societe des Nouvelles Editions Eddie Barclay, Paris, France
Copyright for the U.S.A. and Canada © 1969 Management Agency & Music Publishing, Inc. (BMI)
All Rights Reserved Used by Permission

F
Fm/B♭
each and ev - 'ry high - way. And
step a - long the by - way. And
say, "Not in a shy way." Oh
C
G7
To Coda
3
more, much more than this, I did it
more, much more than this, I did it
no, oh no, not me, I did it
1.
F6
C
2.
F6
My Way. Re - My
C
3
Way. Yes, there were times, I'm sure you
C7
F
knew, when I bit off more than I could
Dm7
chew. But through it all, when there was
G7
Em7
doubt, I ate it up and spit it
Am
Dm7
out. I faced it all, and I stood

G7
F6
C
D.S. al Coda
tall and did it My Way. I've
CODA
F6
C
My Way. For what is a
C7
man, what has he got? If not him -
F
self, then he has not to say the
Dm7
G7
things he tru - ly feels and not the
Em7
Am
words of one who kneels. The rec - ord
Dm7
G7
shows I took the blows and did it
F6
C
G7
C
My Way.

LOVE ME TENDER

Words and Music by
ELVIS PRESLEY and VERA MATSON

Copyright © 1956 by Elvis Presley Music, Inc.
Copyright Renewed and Assigned to Elvis Presley Music (Administered by R&H Music)
International Copyright Secured All Rights Reserved

ONE BROKEN HEART FOR SALE

Words and Music by
OTIS BLACKWELL and WINFIELD SCOTT

Copyright © 1963 by Elvis Presley Music, Inc.
Copyright Renewed and Assigned to Elvis Presley Music (Administered by R&H Music)
International Copyright Secured All Rights Reserved

F
Dm
Since she re - ject - ed me, there's
That girl re - ject - ed me just
She turned and walked a - way and
I think I'll paint a sign: For
To Coda
1., 2.
3.
Bb
C7
F
(D.C.)
F
D.S. al Coda
noth - ing left to save me.
when I thought I had her.
told me I was play - ing.
sale for a
CODA
F
F
pen - ny.
Who wants to
Dm
F
buy a heart?
One bro - ken
Dm
Bb
lov - er's heart,
One Bro - ken
C7
1.
F
Heart
For Sale.
C7
2.
F
Bb7
F
Sale.

ONE NIGHT

Words and Music by
DAVE BARTHOLOMEW and PEARL KING

Copyright © 1957 Travis Music, Inc.
Copyright Renewed and Assigned to Unart Music Corporation
All Rights for the U.S.A. and Canada Assigned to Elvis Presley Music (Administered by R&H Music)
International Copyright Secured All Rights Reserved

F7
Al - ways lived a ver - y qui - et life.
C
I ain't nev - er did no wrong.
D7
Now I know that life with - out you ___ has
G7 N.C. G7#5
been ___ too ___ lone - ly too long. ___ One Night with
C Dm7 G7
you is what I'm now pray - ing for.
Dm7 G7
The things that we two could plan
Dm7 G7 1. C F7
would make my dreams come true.
G7 N.C. 2. C F7 C
One Night with true. ___

(There'll Be) PEACE IN THE VALLEY (For Me)

Words and Music by
THOMAS A. DORSEY

Copyright © 1939 by Thomas A. Dorsey
Copyright Renewed, Assigned to Unichappell Music Inc.
International Copyright Secured All Rights Reserved

F Bb Bbm F Bb
day.
seen.
am.
me.
There'll be Peace In The
F
Val - ley for me some - day. There'll be
G7 C7 G7
Peace In The Val - ley for me. I
C7 F F7
pray no more sor - row and sad - ness or
Bb G7
trou - ble will be. There'll be
F G7 C7
Peace In The Val - ley for
1. - 3.
F Bb Bbm F
me.
There the
There the
No
4.
F Bb Bbm F
me.

THE PROMISED LAND

Words and Music by
CHUCK BERRY

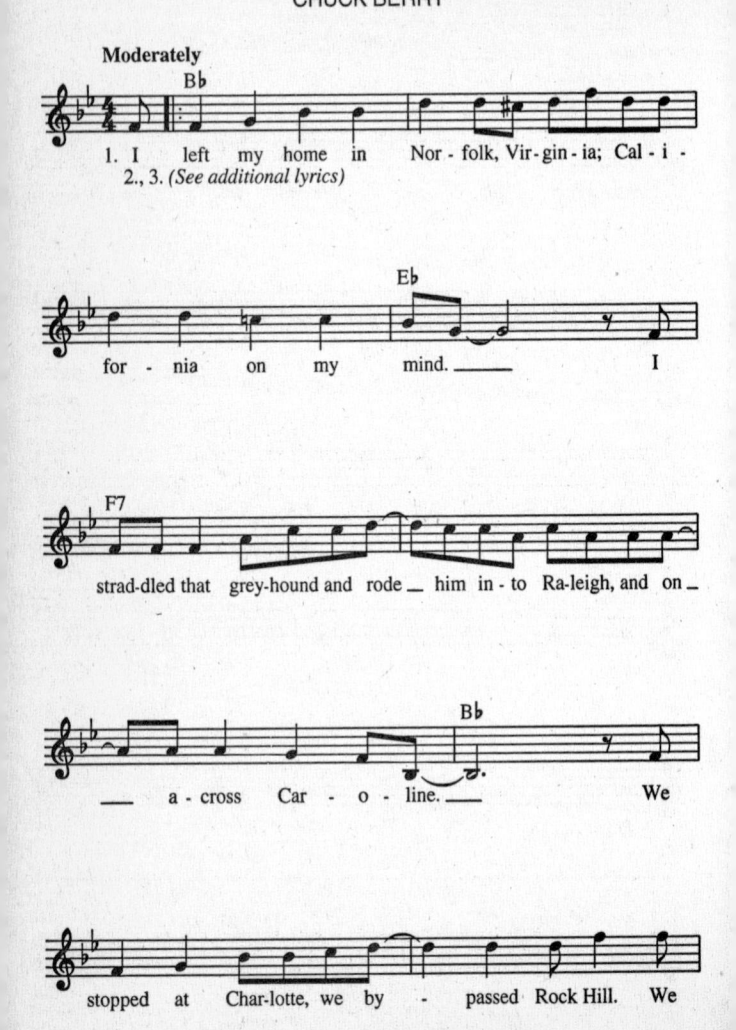

Copyright © 1964 (Renewed) by Arc Music Corporation
International Copyright Secured All Rights Reserved

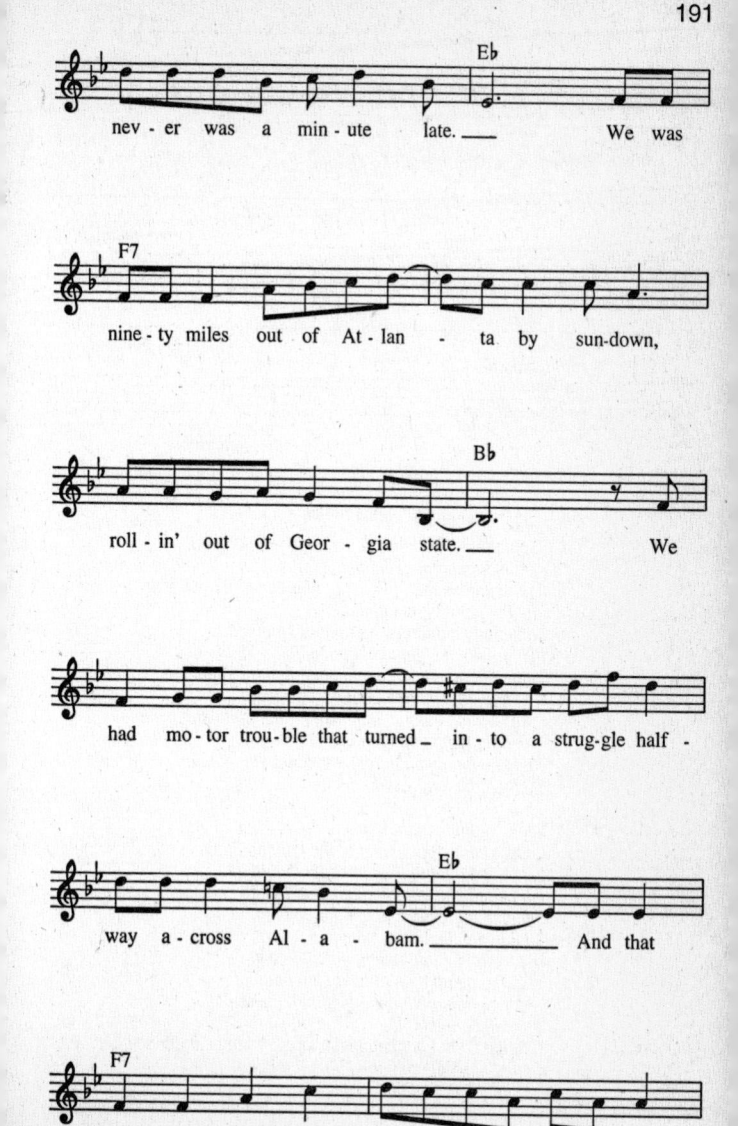
Eb
nev - er was a min - ute late. We was
F7
nine - ty miles out of At - lan - ta by sun-down,
Bb
roll - in' out of Geor - gia state. We
had mo - tor trou - ble that turned in - to a strug-gle half -
Eb
way a - cross Al - a - bam. And that
F7
'hound broke down and left us all strand-ed in

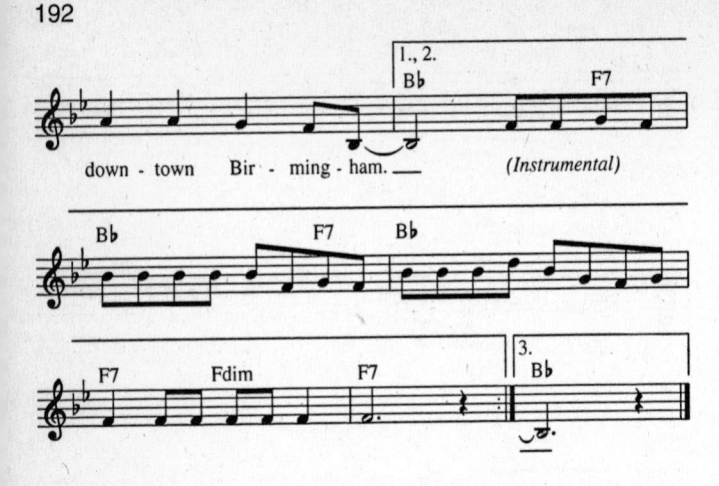

Additional Lyrics

2. Right away I bought me a through train ticket,
Ridin' across Mississippi clean.
And I was on the Midnight Flyer out of Birmingham,
Smokin' into New Orleans.
Somebody helped me get out of Louisiana,
Just to help me get to Houston Town.
There are people there who care a little about me,
And they won't let a poor boy down.
Sure as you're born, they bought me a silk suit,
They put luggage in my hand.
And I woke up high over Albuquerque on a jet
To the Promised Land.

3. Workin' on a T-bone steak,
I had a party flyin' over to the Golden State,
When the pilot told us in thirteen minutes
He would get us at the Terminal Gate.
Swing low, chariot, come down easy,
Taxi to the Terminal Line.
Cut your engines and cool your wings,
And let me make it to the telephone.
Los Angeles, give me Norfolk, Virginia,
Tidewater 4-10-0-0.
Tell the folks back home this is the Promised Land
Callin', and the poor boy's on the line.

SEPARATE WAYS

Words and Music by
RED WEST and RICHARD MAINEGRA

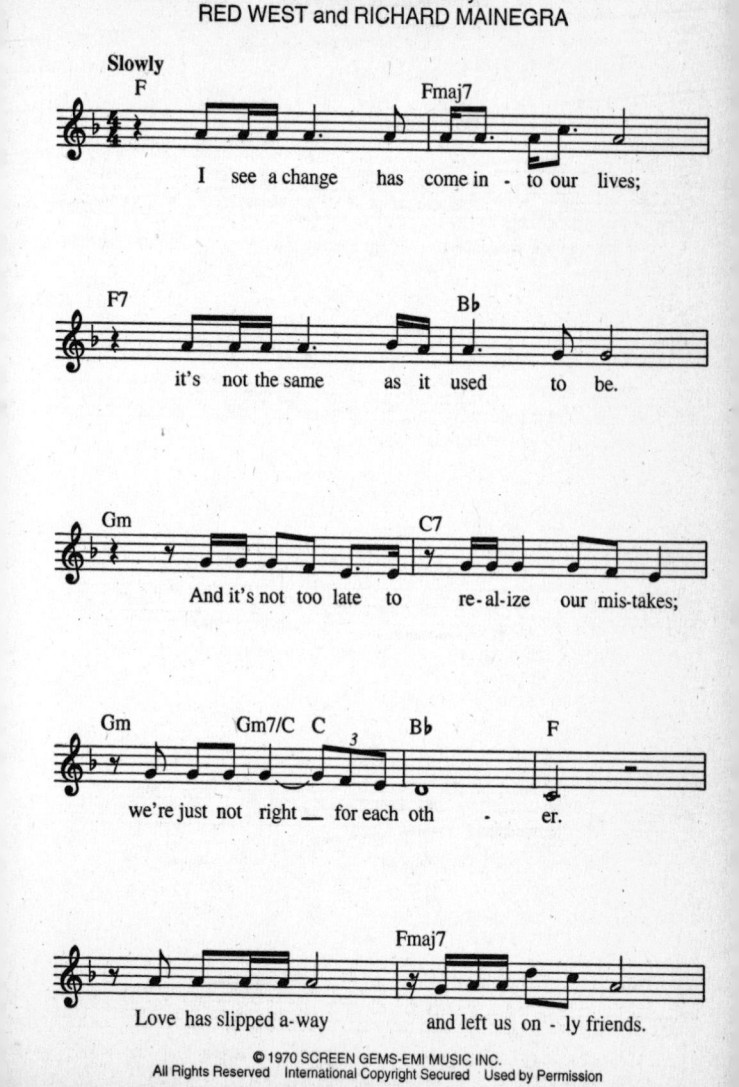

© 1970 SCREEN GEMS-EMI MUSIC INC.
All Rights Reserved International Copyright Secured Used by Permission

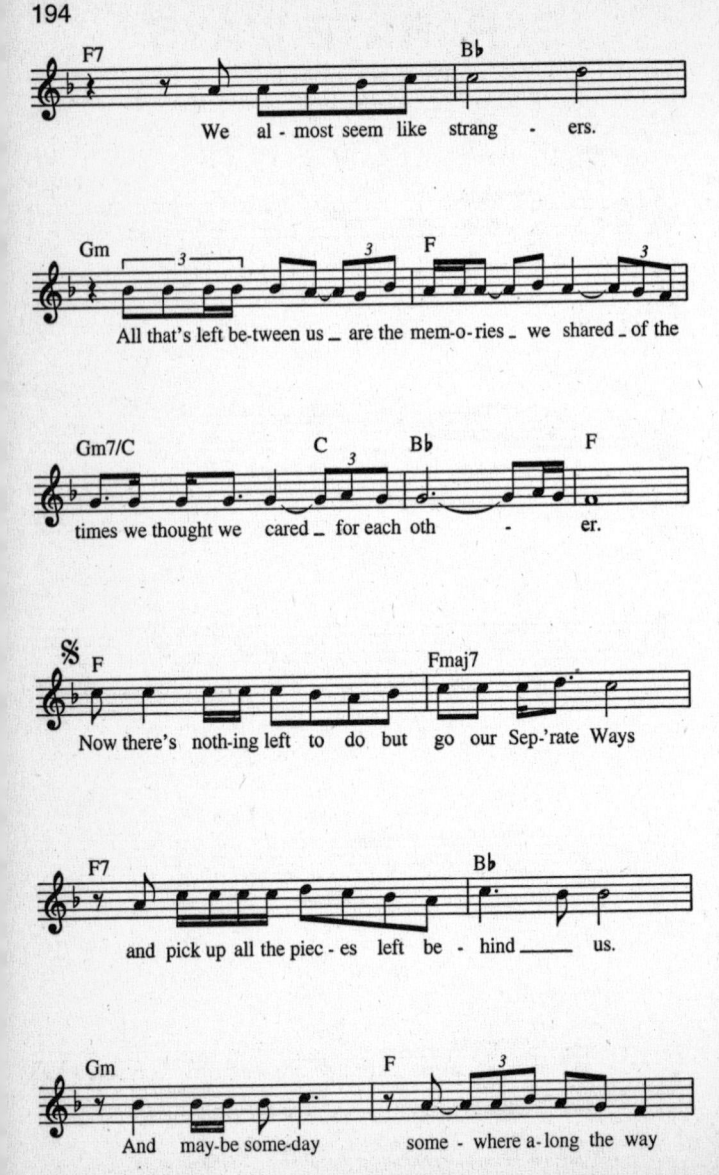
F7
Bb
We al - most seem like strang - ers.
Gm
F
All that's left be-tween us _ are the mem-o-ries _ we shared _ of the
Gm7/C
C
Bb
F
times we thought we cared _ for each oth - er.
F
Fmaj7
Now there's noth-ing left to do but go our Sep-'rate Ways
F7
Bb
and pick up all the piec - es left be - hind _____ us.
Gm
F
And may-be some-day some - where a-long the way

PROPERTY OF
HIGH POINT PUBLIC LIBRARY
HIGH POINT, NORTH CAROLINA

PUPPET ON A STRING

Words and Music by
SID TEPPER and ROY C. BENNETT

Copyright © 1965 by Gladys Music, Inc.
Copyright Renewed and Assigned to Gladys Music (Administered by Williamson Music)
International Copyright Secured All Rights Reserved

C D7 G
dar - ling, please be kind. I
C D7 G Em
of - fer you the tru - est love that
A7 D7 G
you will ev - er find. Take my heart and
Am D7
please be fair, han - dle it with
G G7 C
lov - ing care. For I'm just a
G Am
Pup - pet On A String, and you can do 'most
D7 G
an - y - thing with me.

RETURN TO SENDER

Words and Music by
OTIS BLACKWELL and WINFIELD SCOTT

Copyright © 1962 by Elvis Presley Music, Inc.
Copyright Renewed and Assigned to Elvis Presley Music (Administered by R&H Music)
International Copyright Secured All Rights Reserved

F
G7
D7
a lov-ers' spat.
I write, "I'm
G7
D.C. al Coda
sor - ry," but my let - ter keeps com-ing back.
CODA
C7
F
zone.
This time I'm gon-na take it my - self and
C
D7
put it right in her hand.
And if it comes back the
G7 N.C.
ver-y next day,
then I'll un-der - stand
the writ-ing on it.
F
G7
F
Re - turn
To Send-er,
ad - dress un -
G7
F
G7
known.
No such num-ber,
C
1.
C7
2.
F7
C
no such zone.
zone.

ROCK-A-HULA BABY

Words and Music by BEN WEISMAN,
DOLORES FULLER and FRED WISE

Copyright © 1961 Gladys Music, Inc.
Copyright Renewed, Assigned to Chappell & Co., Bienstock Publishing Company and Erika Publishing
International Copyright Secured All Rights Reserved

Ab7
Eb
a - hu - la Ba - by, Rock -
Ab7
a - hu - la Ba - by. Got a
Ab
Eb
hu - la lu - lu from
Ab
Eb
Hon - o - lu - lu, that
Bb
N.C.
Eb
Rock - a - hu - la Ba - by of mine.
1., 2.
N.C.
3.
Al - though I
I bet that

SHE'S NOT YOU

Words and Music by DOC POMUS,
JERRY LEIBER and MIKE STOLLER

Copyright © 1962 by Elvis Presley Music, Inc.
Copyright Renewed and Assigned to Elvis Presley Music
(Administered by R&H Music), Jerry Leiber Music and Mike Stoller Music
International Copyright Secured All Rights Reserved

PROPERTY OF
HIGH POINT PUBLIC LIBRARY
HIGH POINT, NORTH CAROLINA

SPINOUT

Words and Music by SID WAYNE,
BEN WEISMAN and DARRELL FULLER

Copyright © 1966 by Gladys Music, Inc.
Copyright Assigned to Gladys Music (Administered by Williamson Music)
Copyright Renewed
International Copyright Secured All Rights Reserved

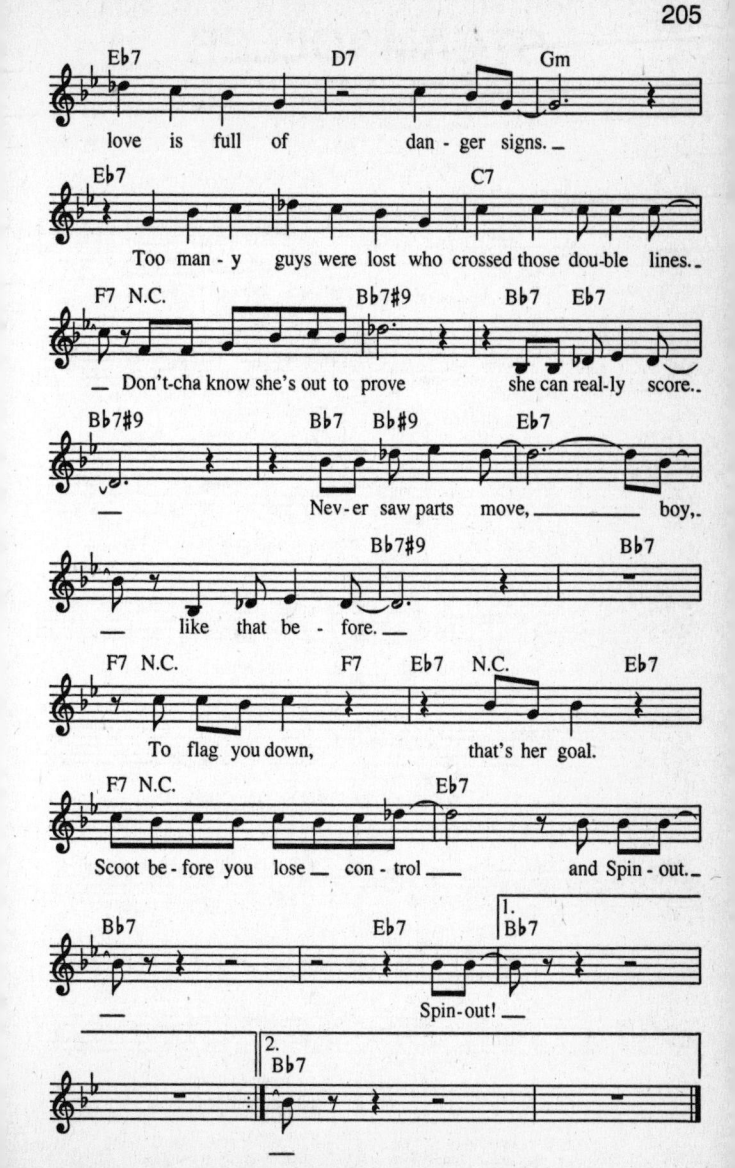
Eb7 D7 Gm
love is full of dan - ger signs.
Eb7 C7
Too man - y guys were lost who crossed those dou-ble lines.
F7 N.C. Bb7#9 Bb7 Eb7
Don't-cha know she's out to prove she can real-ly score..
Bb7#9 Bb7 Bb#9 Eb7
Nev-er saw parts move, boy,.
Bb7#9 Bb7
like that be - fore.
F7 N.C. F7 Eb7 N.C. Eb7
To flag you down, that's her goal.
F7 N.C. Eb7
Scoot be - fore you lose con - trol and Spin - out.
Bb7 Eb7 1. Bb7
Spin-out!
2. Bb7

STEAMROLLER
(Steamroller Blues)

Words and Music by
JAMES TAYLOR

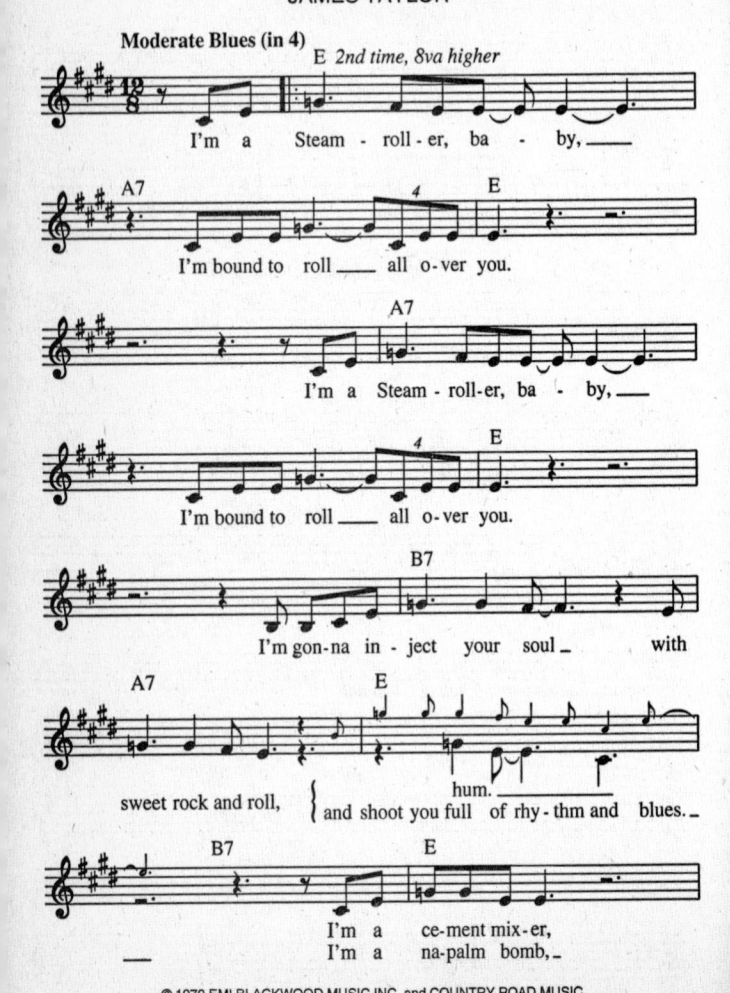

© 1970 EMI BLACKWOOD MUSIC INC. and COUNTRY ROAD MUSIC
All Rights Controlled and Administered by EMI BLACKWOOD MUSIC INC.
All Rights Reserved International Copyright Secured Used by Permission

A7
E
a churn-in' urn of burn - in' funk.
just guar - an - teed to blow your mind.
A7
I'm a ce-ment mix - er,
I'm a na-palm bomb,
E
a churn-in' urn of burn - in' funk.
just guar - an - teed to blow your mind.
B7
I'm a dem - o - li - tion der - by,
If I can't have your love now, ba - by,
A7
4
1.
E
a heft - y hunk of steam-in' junk.
there won't be noth - ing left be-
B7
2.
E
D9 E♭9 E9
I'm a hind.

STUCK ON YOU

Words and Music by
AARON SCHROEDER and J. LESLIE McFARLAND

Copyright © 1960 by Gladys Music, Inc.
Copyright Renewed and Assigned to Gladys Music (Administered by Williamson Music)
and Rachel's Own Music (Administered by A. Schroeder International Ltd.)
International Copyright Secured All Rights Reserved

F
Ain't gon - na do you no good at all. 'Cause
B♭
once I catch ya and the kiss - in' starts, a
C7 N.C.
team o' wild hors - es could-n't tear us a - part.
F
Try to take a ti - ger from his dad-dy's side.
That's how love is gon - na keep us tied. Uh-huh - huh.
B♭7
F
Yes-sir - ee, uh - huh.
C7
C7#5
I'm gon - na stick like glue,
B♭7
F N.C.
F
yay, yay, be-cause I'm Stuck On You.

SURRENDER

Original Italian Lyrics by G.B. De CURTIS
English Words and Adaptation by
DOC POMUS and MORT SHUMAN
Music by E. De CURTIS

Copyright (for the U.S.A.) © 1960 by Elvis Presley Music, Inc.
Copyright (for the U.S.A.) Renewed and Assigned to Elvis Presley Music (Administered by R&H Music);
rights for all countries in the world (except U.S.A.) owned by Edizioni Bideri S.p.A, Naples
International Copyright Secured All Rights Reserved

C
ten - der. Let me
Dm7
hold you in my arms, dear,
G7
G7♯5
C
while the moon shines bright a - bove.
D♯dim
C
N.C.
All the stars will tell the
Dm7
G7
sto - ry of our
E7
Am
love and all its glo - ry.
Fm
Cm
Let us take this night of mag - ic
G7
A♭7
G7
and make it a night of

Cm
N.C.
love.
Won't you please Sur -
Dm7
G7
ren - der to me
your lips, your
G7#5
C
arms, your heart, dear.
Fm6
Cm
Be mine for - ev -
G7
Fm6
er; be mine to -
1.
Cm
A♭7
G7 N.C.
(D.C.)
2.
Cm
night!
night!
Fm
Cm

TREAT ME NICE

Words and Music by
JERRY LEIBER and MIKE STOLLER

© 1957 (Renewed) JERRY LEIBER MUSIC and MIKE STOLLER MUSIC
All Rights Reserved

C7
it's not fair to tease. So
F
if you come on cold, I'm
real - ly gon - na freeze. If you
G7 C D7
don't want me to be cold as ice,
G7 N.C. C C7
Treat Me Nice.
F C
Make me feel at home
F F#dim C
if you real - ly care.
F C C+
Scratch my back and run your pret - ty

F
F♯
G7
fin - gers through my hair. You
C
know I'd be your slave
C7
if you ask me to. But
F
if you don't be - have, I'll
walk right out on you. If you
G7
want my love then take my ad -
D7
G7 N.C.
1.
C
F7
vice:
Treat Me Nice.
G7
2.
C
F7
C
When Nice.

SUSPICIOUS MINDS

Words and Music by
MARK JAMES

© 1968 (Renewed 1996) SCREEN GEMS-EMI MUSIC INC.
All Rights Reserved International Copyright Secured Used by Permission

D C Bm D7 C
say? cry - ing.
We can't go on
G Bm
to - geth - er with Sus - pi - cious Minds,
C D Em Bm
and we can't build our dreams
C
1. (D.C.) D D7
2. B7sus B7
on Sus-pi-cious Minds. Minds.
Slowly
Em Bm C
Oh, let our love sur-vive or dry the
D Em Bm
tears from your eyes. Let's don't let a good thing die
C D G
when, hon-ey, you know I've nev-er lied to you,
Tempo I D.C. and Fade
C G D7 C/D (Lyric 1)
mmm, yeah, yeah!

(Let Me Be Your)
TEDDY BEAR

Words and Music by
KAL MANN and BERNIE LOWE

Copyright © 1957 by Gladys Music, Inc.
Copyright Renewed and Assigned to Gladys Music (Administered by Williamson Music)
International Copyright Secured All Rights Reserved

F
G7
C
li - ons ain't the kind you love e - nough.
N.C.
C
Just wan - na be your Ted - dy
Bear. Put a chain a -
F
round my neck and lead me an - y - where. Oh, let me
C
G7
N.C.
1.
C
F7
be your Ted - dy Bear.
C
G7
(D.C.)
2.
C
F7
C
Bear.

THAT'S ALL RIGHT

Words and Music by
ARTHUR CRUDUP

Copyright © 1947 by Unichappell Music Inc. and Crudup Music
Copyright Renewed
All Rights Administered by Unichappell Music Inc.
International Copyright Secured All Rights Reserved

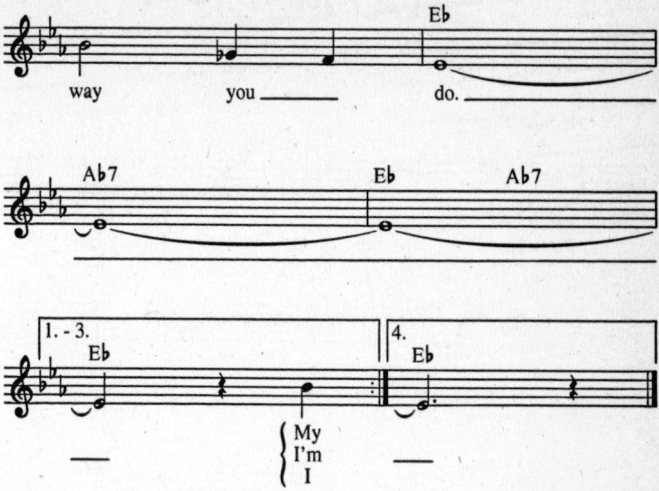

Additional Lyrics

3. I'm leavin' town tomorrow, leavin' town for sure.
   Then you won't be bothered with me hangin' 'round your door.
   But That's All Right, That's All Right.
   That's All Right, Mama, any way you do.

4. I oughta mind my papa; guess I'm not too smart.
   If I was I'd leave you, go before you break my heart.
   But That's All Right, That's All Right.
   That's All Right, Mama, any way you do.

TOO MUCH

Words and Music by
LEE ROSENBERG and BERNIE WEINMAN

Copyright © 1956 by Elvis Presley Music, Inc. and Southern Belle Music
Copyright Renewed and Assigned to Elvis Presley Music
(Administered by R&H Music) and Southern Belle Music
International Copyright Secured All Rights Reserved

1.
N.C.
Much.
2., 3.
N.C.
Much.
Much.
Bb
Need_ your_ lov - in'
all the time._
Need_ your__ hug - gin',
Eb7
please, be mine._
Need_ you__ near me,
Bb
stay real close._
Please,_ please,_ hear me,
F7
you're the most._
Now you got me start-ed, don't you
To Coda
Eb7
Bb
leave me bro-ken-heart-ed 'cause I love you Too
D.C. al Coda
(take 2nd ending)
N.C.
Much.
CODA
Bb
love you Too Much.

T-R-O-U-B-L-E

Words and Music by
JERRY CHESNUT

Copyright © 1975 Sony/ATV Songs LLC
All Rights Administered by Sony/ATV Music Publishing, 8 Music Square West, Nashville, TN 37203
International Copyright Secured All Rights Reserved

G7
D7
E.
What in the world you do-in'
C7
G7
A - L - O - N - E?
Say,
C7
G7
hey, good L - dou-ble - O - K - I - N - G,
D7
C7
I smell T - R - O - U - B - L -
G7
E.
G7
Gm
2. I was a lit - tle bit - ty ba - by when my
3., 4. (See additional lyrics)
pa - pa hit the skids.
Ma - ma had a time tryin' to

raise nine kids. Told me not to stare 'cause it was
G7
im - po - lite. And did the best she could to try to
C7
raise me right. But Ma - ma nev - er told me 'bout - a
G7
no - thin' like - a Y - O - U.
D7
Say, your moth - er must - a been an - oth - er
C7
G
some-thin' or an - oth - er, too.
C7
Say, hey, good L - dou-ble - O - K - I - N -

Additional Lyrics

3. Well, you talk about a woman, I've seen a lotta others
With too much somethin' and not enough of another,
Lookin' like glory and walkin' like a dream.
Mother Nature's sure been good to Y-O-U.
Well, your mother musta been another good lookin' mother, too.
Say, hey! Good L-double O-K-I-N-G, I smell T-R-O-U-B-L-E.

4. Well, you talk about a trouble makin' hunka' pokey bait
The men are gonna love and all the women gonna hate.
Remindin' them of everything, they're never gonna be,
Maybe the beginnin' of a World War Three,
'Cause the world ain't ready for nothing like a Y-O-U.
I bet your mother musta been another somethin' or the other, too.
Say, hey! Good L-double O-K-I-N-G, I smell T-R-O-U-B-L-E.

UNCHAINED MELODY

Lyric by HY ZARET
Music by ALEX NORTH

© 1955 (Renewed) FRANK MUSIC CORP.
All Rights Reserved

To Coda
D7
G
to
me!
A little faster
C
D
C
Lone - ly riv - ers flow to the sea, to the
Lone - ly moun-tains gaze at the stars, at the
B♭
C
D
sea, to the o - pen arms of the
stars, wait - ing for the dawn of the
G
C
sea. Lone - ly riv - ers
day. All a - lone, I
D
C
B♭
sigh, "Wait for me, wait for me!"
gaze at the stars, at the stars,
C
D
1.
G
I'll be com - ing home, wait for me!
dream - ing of my love far a -
(D.C.)
2.
G
D.C. al Coda
way.
CODA
G
Em
Cmaj7
Am7
G
me!

UNTIL IT'S TIME FOR YOU TO GO

Words and Music by
BUFFY SAINTE-MARIE

Copyright © 1965, 1967 by Gypsy Boy Music, Inc.
Copyright Renewed
International Copyright Secured All Rights Reserved

Cmaj7 Em7♭5 A7
part, we're not the same. We laughed and
Dm7 Dm(maj7) Dm7♭5
played at the start like in a game.
G7 C Cmaj7
You could have stayed out-side my heart, but in you
Gm6 A7 Dm7
came. And here you'll stay Un - til It's
G7 C Fm7
Time For You To Go.
G7 C Fm7 G7
Don't ask why. Don't ask
C B7 E7
how. Don't ask for -
Am D7 Asus D7
ev - er; love me
CODA
G7 D.S. al Coda C
now! This love of Go.

VIVA LAS VEGAS

Words and Music by
DOC POMUS and MORT SHUMAN

Copyright © 1964 by Elvis Presley Music, Inc.
Copyright Renewed 1992 by Sharyn Felder and Geoffrey J. Felder on
behalf of Doc Pomus and Mort Shuman Songs on behalf of Mort Shuman
All Rights for Sharyn Felder and Geoffrey J. Felder in the United States Administered by Pomus Songs, Inc.
All Rights for Mort Shuman Songs in the United States Administered by Warner-Tamerlane Publishing Corp.
All Rights for the world outside the United States Controlled by Elvis Presley Music (Administerd by R&H Music)
International Copyright Secured All Rights Reserved

liv - in', dev - il may care. And
lost on ev - 'ry deal.
I'm just the dev - il with love to spare.
All you need's a strong heart and a nerve of steel.
C
G
Vi - va Las Ve - gas,
Vi - va Las Ve - gas,
1.
C
G
Vi - va Las Ve - gas.
Vi - va Las
(D.C.)
2.
G
C
Ve - gas. Vi - va Las
Ve - gas with your ne - on flash - in' and your
G
one arm ban - dits crash - in'; all those hopes
C
down the drain. Vi - va Las
Ve - gas turn - in' day in - to night-time, turn - in'

A7
night in - to day - time. If you see it once,
you'll nev - er be the same a - gain.
D7
G D7
I'm gon - na
G
keep on the run, I'm gon - na have me some
fun if it costs me my ver - y last
dime. If I wind up broke,
well, I'll al - ways re - mem - ber that I
B7
had a swing - in' time.
Em
I'm gon - na give it ev - 'ry - thing I've got.

La - dy Luck, please let the
dice stay hot. Let me shoot a
C
sev - en with ev - 'ry shot. Vi - va
G
C
Las Ve - gas, Vi - va
G
C
Las Ve - gas, Vi - va
G
C
Las Ve - gas, Vi - va,
D7
G
Vi - va Las Ve - gas
G6
Gmaj7
G

WALK A MILE IN MY SHOES

Words and Music by
JOE SOUTH

Copyright © 1969 by Lowery Music Co., Inc.
All Rights Reserved Used by Permission

Additional Lyrics

2. Now your whole world you see around you is just a reflection,
   And the law of karma says you reap just what you sow.
   So, unless you've lived a life of total perfection,
   You'd better be careful of every stone that you should throw.
   (Chorus)

3. And yet we spend the day throwing stones at one another,
   'Cause I don't think or wear my hair the same way you do.
   Well, I may be common people, but I'm your brother.
   And when you strike out and try to hurt me it's a-hurtin' you.
   (Chorus)

4. There are people on reservations and out in the ghettos,
   And, brother, there but for the grace of God go you and I.
   If I only had the wings of a little angel,
   Don't you know I'd fly to the top of the mountain and then I'd cry?
   (Chorus)

WAY DOWN

Words and Music by
LAYNG MARTINE, JR.

Moderately, with a strong beat

Copyright © 1977 by Ray Stevens Music
International Copyright Secured All Rights Reserved

feel it, feel it, feel it.
(Way
G7
C
Way Down where the mu - sic plays,
Way Down like a
Down!)
(Way Down!)
G7
ti - dal wave.
Way Down where the fires blaze, Way
(Way Down!)
F
C
F/A
C/G
Down,
down,
F
C
G7
C
To Coda
way, way on down.
(Way on down.)
(D.C.)
3
3
3
(Instrumental)
C
Hold me a-gain as tight as you can. I need you so, ba-
CODA
D.S. al Coda
- by, let's go!
down, way on down.)

YOU'VE LOST THAT LOVIN' FEELIN'

Words and Music by BARRY MANN,
CYNTHIA WEIL and PHIL SPECTOR

© 1964, 1965 (Renewed 1992, 1993) SCREEN GEMS-EMI MUSIC INC. and MOTHER BERTHA MUSIC, INC.
All Rights on behalf of MOTHER BERTHA MUSIC, INC. Administered by ABKCO MUSIC, INC.
All Rights Reserved International Copyright Secured Used by Permission

Bb/C
1. C
gone, gone, gone, woh oh oh oh.
2. C F G F G
Now there's no
C F G F G
Ba - by, ba - by, I'd get down on my knees for
C F G F G C F
you if that would make you
G F G C F
love me like you used to do.
G/F G C F G F G
We had a love, a love, a love you don't find ev-'ry
C F G F G C F
day. So don't, don't,
G F G C 3 F G F G
don't, don't let it slip a - way.
C F G F G 3
Ba - by, ba - by, I beg you
(Bkgd:) Ba - by, ba - by,

C F G F G
please, please, I need your
beg you please, please,
C F G F G
love, I need your love, so bring it on
I need your love, I need your love,
C F G
back, so bring it on back.
bring it on back, bring it on back.
C Dm/C G7
Bring back that lov - in' feel - in', woh oh, that lov -
C Dm/C
- in' feel - in'. Bring back that lov - in' feel - in', 'cause it's
B♭/C
gone, gone, gone, and I can't go
C
Repeat and Fade
on, woh oh oh oh.

WEAR MY RING AROUND YOUR NECK

Words and Music by
BERT CARROLL and RUSSELL MOODY

Copyright © 1958 (Renewed) and Assigned to Lollipop Music Corp. for the U.S.A.
All Rights for the rest of the world controlled by Elvis Presley Music, Inc. (administered by R&H Music), Pinelawn Music Publishing Co., Inc. and Tideland Music Publishing Corp.
International Copyright Secured All Rights Reserved

C7
F7
They say that go - ing stead - y is
C
C7
F7
not the prop - er thing. They say that we're too
C
C7
young to know the mean - ing of a ring. I
F7
on - ly know I love ___ you and
C
D7
that you love me, too. So, dar - ling, please do
G7
D7♭5
G7
N.C.
what I ask of you. _____ Won't you Wear My

C
Ring A - round Your Neck
to tell the world I'm yours, by
G7
C
heck?
Let them see
Let them know
C7
F
your love for me, and let them
I love you so, and let them
C
G7 N.C.
1.
C F7
see
know
by the ring a - round your neck.
G7 N.C.
2.
C F7 C
Won't you Wear My neck.

THE WONDER OF YOU

Words and Music by
BAKER KNIGHT

Slowly, with expression

F Dm

When no one else can un - der - stand me,
And when you smile, the world is bright - er.
You'll nev - er know how much I love you.

Gm7 C7

when ev - 'ry - thing I do is wrong,
You touch my hand and I'm a king.
My love is yours and yours a - lone,

F Dm

you give me love and con - so - la - tion.
Your kiss to me is worth a for - tune.
and it's so won - der - ful to have you,

Gm7 C7

You give me hope to car - ry on, and you
Your love to me is ev - 'ry - thing, and you're
to have you for my ver - y own. Guess I'll

© Copyright 1958, 1964 by DUCHESS MUSIC CORPORATION
Copyright Renewed
DUCHESS MUSIC CORPORATION is an MCA company
International Copyright Secured All Rights Reserved
MCA music publishing

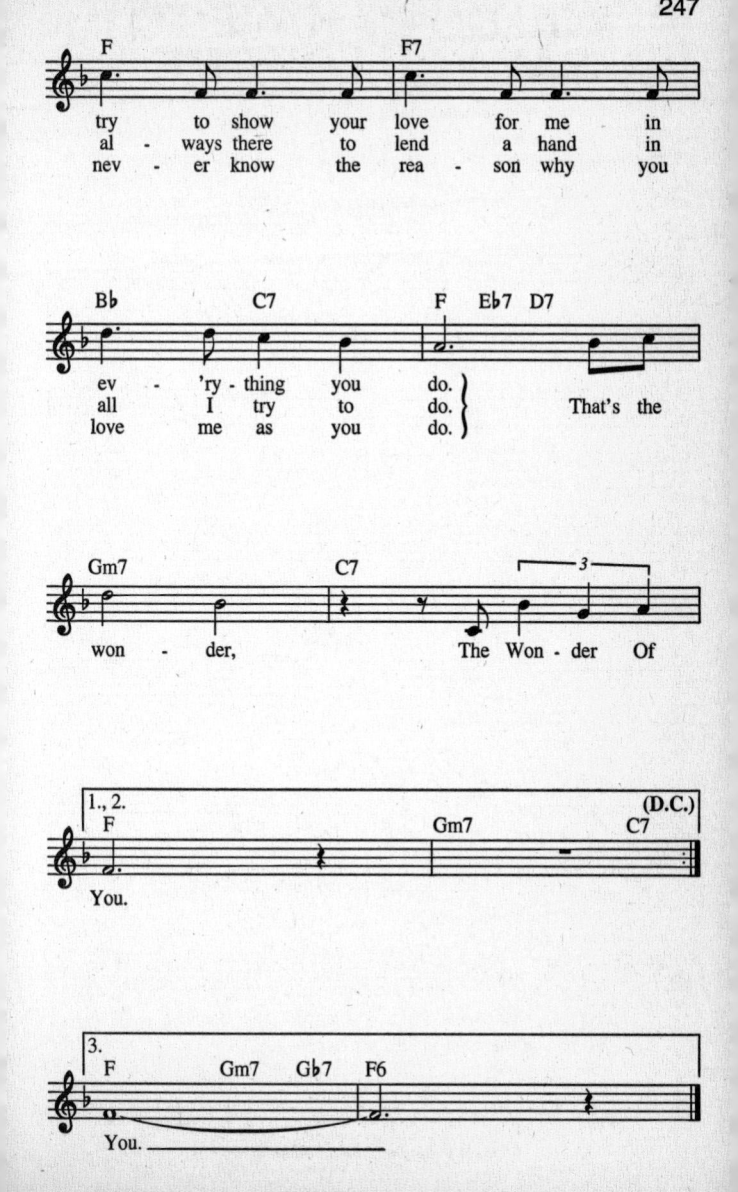
F
F7
try to show your love for me in
al - ways there to lend a hand in
nev - er know the rea - son why you
B♭
C7
F
E♭7
D7
ev - 'ry - thing you do.
all I try to do.
love me as you do.
That's the
Gm7
C7
3
won - der,
The Won - der Of
1., 2.
(D.C.)
F
Gm7
C7
You.
3.
F
Gm7
G♭7
F6
You.

YOU DON'T HAVE TO SAY YOU LOVE ME

Music by P. DONAGGIO
Italian Lyrics by V. PALLAVICINI
English Lyrics by VICKI WICKHAM and SIMON NAPIER-BELL

Copyright © 1965, 1966 ACCORDO EDIZIONI MUSICALI, Milan, Italy
Copyrights Renewed
Rights in the United States, Canada, British Commonwealth of Nations, South Africa, Korea, China and Taiwan Controlled by EMI MILLER CATALOG INC. (Publishing) and WARNER BROS. PUBLICATIONS U.S. INC. (Print)
All Rights Reserved Used by Permission

F Dm Gm C7
You Don't Have To Say You Love Me, just be close at hand.
To Coda
F Dm Gm7 C7
You don't have to stay for-ev - er; I will un-der-stand. Be-
F Am Dm
lieve me, be-lieve me, I can't help but love you. But be-
Gm7 C
lieve me, I'll nev - er tie you down.
D.S. al Coda
CODA
N.C. F
Left a-lone with just a lieve me, be-
D G Em
lieve me. You Don't Have To Say You Love Me,
Am D7 G Em
just be close at hand. You don't have to stay for-ev - er;
Am7 D7 G Dm6
I will un-der-stand. Be-lieve me, be-
G Dm6 G
lieve me, be-lieve me.

YOU'RE THE DEVIL IN DISGUISE

Words and Music by BILL GIANT,
BERNIE BAUM and FLORENCE KAYE

Copyright © 1963 by Elvis Presley Music, Inc.
Copyright Renewed and Assigned to Elvis Presley Music (Administered by R&H Music)
International Copyright Secured All Rights Reserved

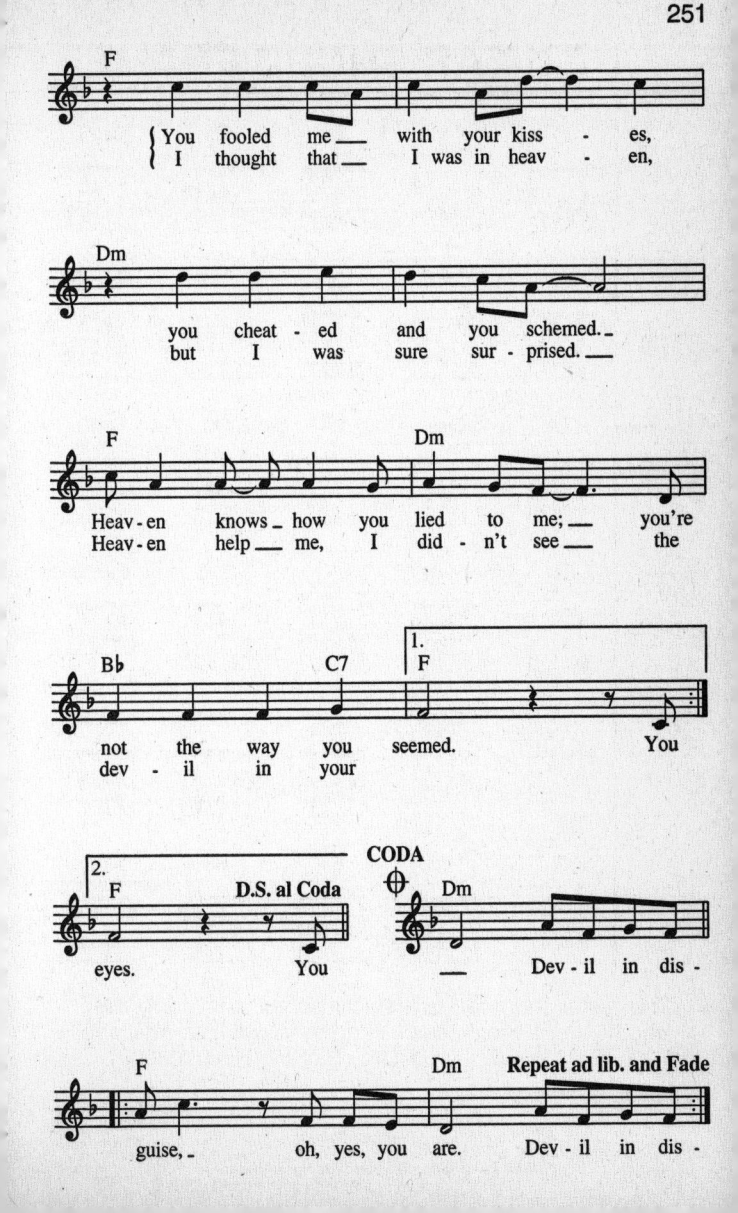
F
You fooled me with your kiss - es,
I thought that I was in heav - en,
Dm
you cheat - ed and you schemed.
but I was sure sur - prised.
F
Dm
Heav - en knows how you lied to me; you're
Heav - en help me, I did - n't see the
Bb
C7
1.
F
not the way you seemed. You
dev - il in your
2.
F
D.S. al Coda
eyes. You
CODA
Dm
Dev - il in dis -
F
Dm
Repeat ad lib. and Fade
guise, oh, yes, you are. Dev - il in dis -

GUITAR CHORD FRAMES

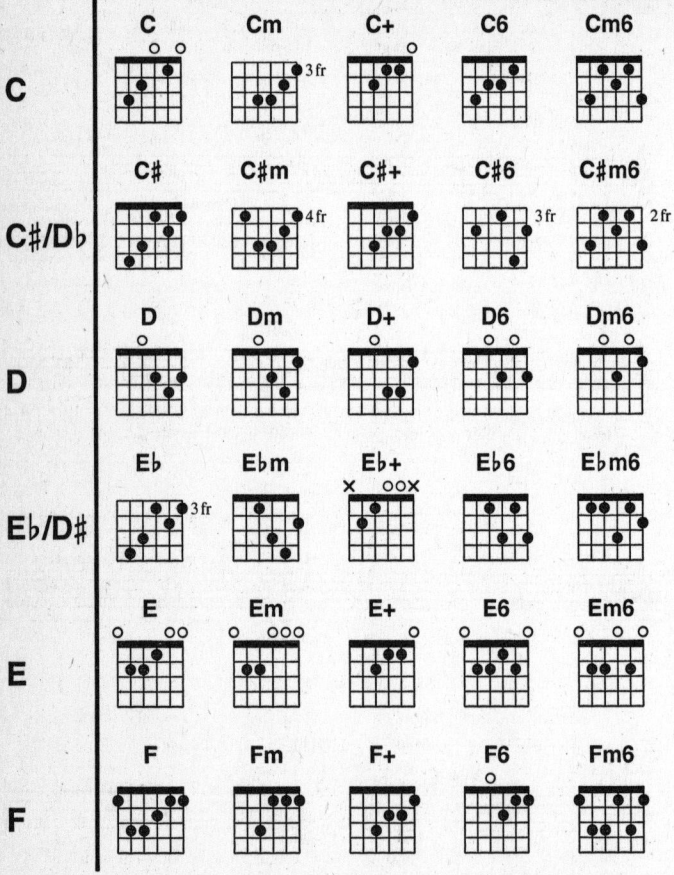

This guitar chord reference includes 120 commonly used chords. For a more complete guide to guitar chords, see "THE PAPERBACK CHORD BOOK" (HL00702009).

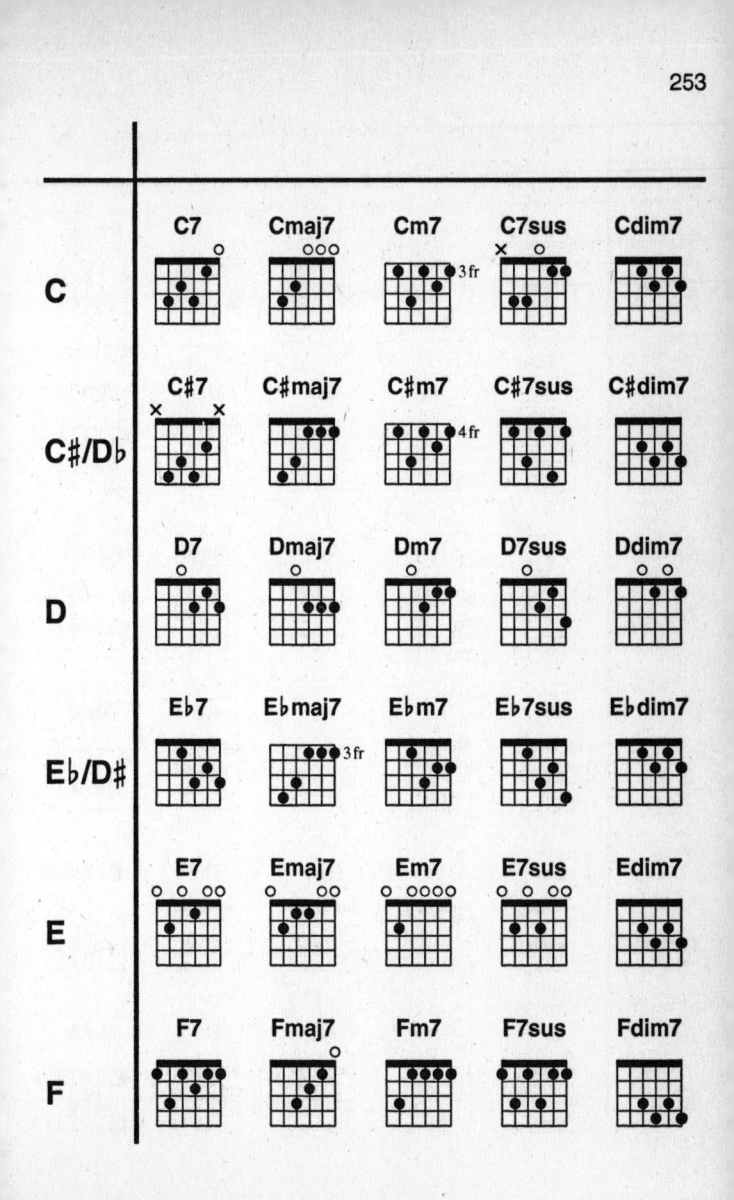
C
C7
Cmaj7
Cm7
3fr
C7sus
Cdim7
C♯/D♭
C♯7
C♯maj7
C♯m7
4fr
C♯7sus
C♯dim7
D
D7
Dmaj7
Dm7
D7sus
Ddim7
E♭/D♯
E♭7
E♭maj7
3fr
E♭m7
E♭7sus
E♭dim7
E
E7
Emaj7
Em7
E7sus
Edim7
F
F7
Fmaj7
Fm7
F7sus
Fdim7

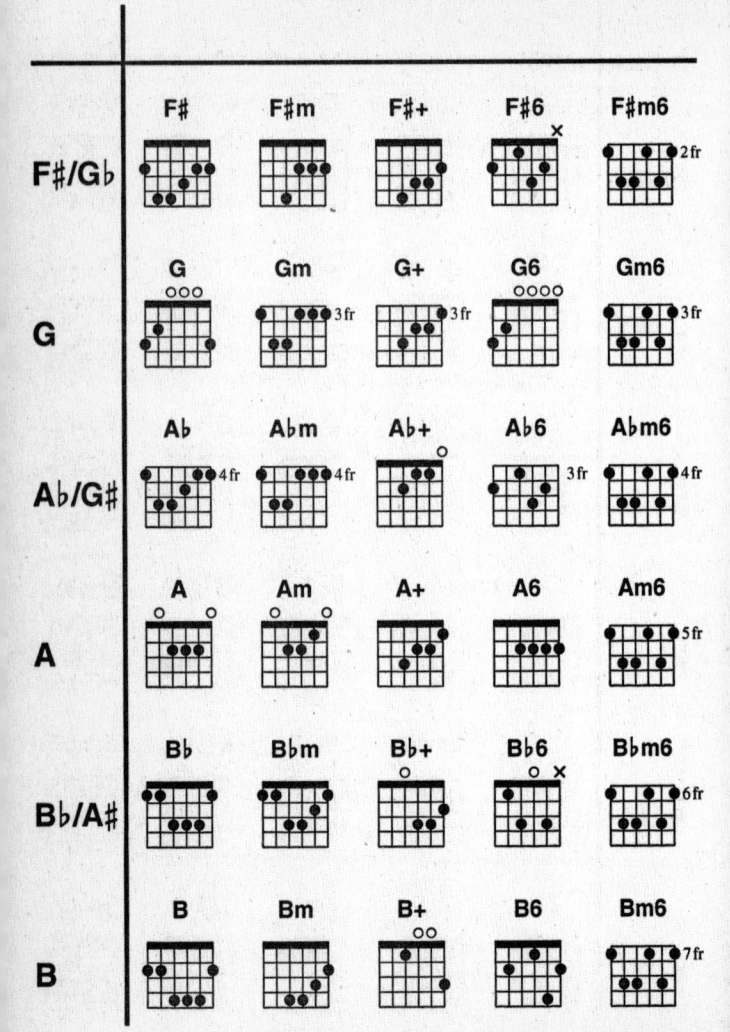
F♯/G♭
F♯
F♯m
F♯+
F♯6
F♯m6
2fr
G
G
Gm
3fr
G+
3fr
G6
Gm6
3fr
A♭/G♯
A♭
A♭m
4fr
A♭+
A♭6
3fr
A♭m6
4fr
A
A
Am
A+
A6
Am6
5fr
B♭/A♯
B♭
B♭m
B♭+
B♭6
B♭m6
6fr
B
B
Bm
B+
B6
Bm6
7fr

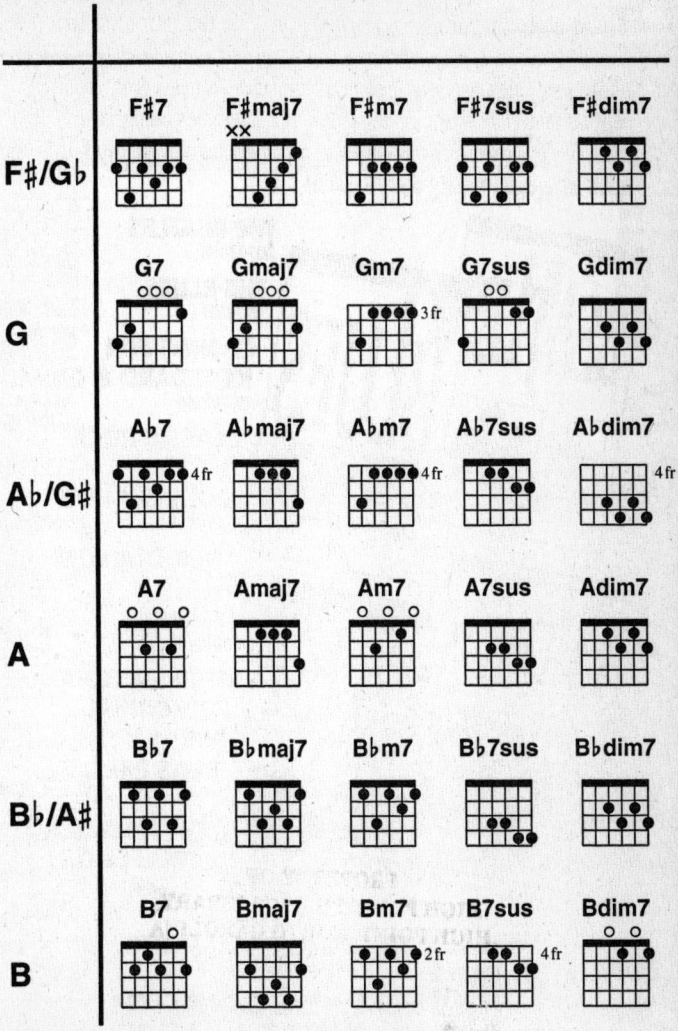
F♯/G♭
F♯7
F♯maj7
F♯m7
F♯7sus
F♯dim7
G
G7
Gmaj7
Gm7
3 fr
G7sus
Gdim7
A♭/G♯
A♭7
4 fr
A♭maj7
A♭m7
4 fr
A♭7sus
A♭dim7
4 fr
A
A7
Amaj7
Am7
A7sus
Adim7
B♭/A♯
B♭7
B♭maj7
B♭m7
B♭7sus
B♭dim7
B
B7
Bmaj7
Bm7
2 fr
B7sus
4 fr
Bdim7

THE PAPERBACK SONGS SERIES

These perfectly portable paperbacks include the melodies, lyrics, and chords symbols for your favorite songs, all in a convenient, pocket-sized book. Using concise, one-line music notation, anyone from hobbyists to professionals can strum on the guitar, play melodies on the piano, or sing the lyrics to great songs. Books also include a helpful guitar chord chart. A fantastic deal – only $5.95 each!

781.66 L581E c.1
Elvis : melody line, chords
and lyrics for keyboard,

GUITAR

CLASSIC ROCK
00310058

COUNTRY HITS
00702013

NEIL DIAMOND
00702012

HYMNS
00240103

INTERNATIONAL FOLKSONGS
00240104

ELVIS PRESLEY
00240102

THE ROCK & ROLL COLLECTION
00702020

PROPERTY OF
HIGH POINT PUBLIC LIBRARY
HIGH POINT, NORTH CAROLINA

For More Information, See Your Local Music Dealer, Or Write To:

7777 W. Bluemound Rd. P.O. Box 13819 Milwaukee, WI 53213

Prices, availability and contents subject to change without notice.
Some products may not be available outside the U.S.A.

1296